DARK PSYCHOLOGY

Master The Art Of Persuasion and Manipulation: The Ultimate Guide To Improving Your Emotional Intelligence | Improve Your Social Skills For Leadership and Expand Your Influence On Human Behavior

Table of Contents

Introduction

Many films produced in the 1990s and early 2000s featured an Executive level leader who was ruthless. Regardless of gender, they were willing to do whatever needed doing, at anyone's expense to get to the end goal. Think of films like 'The Devil Wears Prada' or 'The Iron Lady.' It was clear who the boss was and that what they said was final.

Art, of course, mimics society. While the argument is not that every office was like that, it is undoubtedly true that the model of leadership was reflected in many organizations, big or small.

As it is now, new leaders are beginning to embrace a human-centered approach to leadership. The idea is simple – that when employees feel connected to the vision of the company they work for, they feel a sense of belonging. They come to believe that they are more than their production value and so they give more of themselves to work, improving results, and work environments.

A leader with a high emotional intelligence score can motivate employees. They can create broad thought processes and improve how information is processed throughout the company. Such a leader can navigate complex decision making in their business based on how well they have mastered emotional response.

Emotional intelligence refers to one's ability to manage their emotions and those of other people.

It includes skills like emotional awareness, emotional management, and the ability to harness emotions to apply them to everyday problem solving and living.

This book argues for the need to develop one's emotional intelligence. It provides scientific backing, which sets up the backdrop for developing one's skills. It then offers practical ways that you can improve your emotional intelligence, arguing that the move will help you, not just in your leadership positions, but even in life as a whole.

Chapter 1: Dark psychology

The importance of dark psychology

It is said of knowledge that it is power. If then that is true, knowing how the human mind works is akin to having superpowers. Psychology is about understanding the workings of the human mind. It is a topic that is central to human existence.

Psychology underpins all things from crime and religion to finance and advertising. It explains complex emotions like love and hate. A person who understands the principles behind the human mind holds in their hand, influence.

Obtaining this knowledge is sometimes hard. Like many of man's advanced secrets, psychological knowledge is buried in dense academic tomes and journals that the general public has no access to. For one to distill this information, they have to delve into countless journals and books, trying to separate what is useful and what they do not need.

Meanwhile, dark psychology is working in the world. This is a fact that you cannot change, even if you do not like it. The choice then becomes whether to maintain your ignorance and risk becoming a victim or to control your situation and learn how to self-preserve and how to protect the people you love from psychological exploitation.

Dark psychology is not just a defense mechanism. There are principles and ideas contained in dark psychology that you can learn to harness to grow in your professional and personal endeavors.

What then is dark psychology?

Dark psychology is the science and art of mind control and manipulation. While psychology itself studies human behavior, dark psychology is about the tactics that people use to manipulate, persuade, coerce and motivate others so that they get what they want.

Criminologists and psychologists use 'The Dark Triad' to pinpoint and predict criminal behavior and to understand broken and problematic relationships.

The Dark Triad

You are unlikely to hear of the Dark Triad in workplaces, but it is one of the 'buzzwords' in psychology. It refers to three personality traits, including psychopathy, Machiavellianism, and narcissism.

- **Narcissism** – The word comes from the Greek mythology of Narcissus, a hunter who started to love his reflection so much as seen in a pool of water that he drowned, staring at himself. Narcissistic people are boastful, selfish, hypersensitive to criticism, and lacking in empathy.
- **Machiavellianism** – The word is derived from the 16th-century Italian diplomat and politician Niccolo Machiavelli. He became known for his book 'The Prince' that has since become an endorsement of the dark arts of deceit and cunning in diplomacy. Traits associated with this personality include self-interest, manipulation, a lack of morality and emotion, and duplicity.
- **Psychopathy** – Traits associated with psychopathy are such as a lack of remorse and empathy, being volatile and manipulative, and antisocial behavior. However, there are differences between a psychopath and having psychopathic traits, as will be discussed later in this chapter.

Narcissism

Narcissism is considered a personality disorder. It is a mental condition where the person has an inflated sense of their importance, troubled relationships, a lack of empathy for others, and a deep need for excessive admiration and attention. Beneath this mask of confidence is fragile self-esteem that cannot survive criticism.

A person with this disorder will cause problems everywhere – at work, in school, with financial affairs, and with relationships. Such people are disappointed and unhappy when they do not get special admiration or favors as they believe themselves to deserve. They find their relationships unfulfilling and cause other people not to want to be around them.

Relationships with narcissists have them expecting constant admiration and attention but without ever seeming to care for the feelings and needs of others. They imagine themselves to be better than other people and to be deserving of such a treatment. They dish out condescension and insults, but they cannot take any whiff of criticism or disagreement.

Note that narcissism does not mean self-love, in the genuine sense. It means a grandiose image of self that allows narcissists to avoid feelings of insecurity. These people are resistant to changing their behavior even when it is the cause of their problems. They blame others instead and react badly to perceived slights.

Symptoms and signs of the disorder

- *A grandiose sense of self-importance*

Narcissists are defined by grandiosity. It goes beyond vanity and arrogance. It is an unrealistic sense of superiority as these people believe that they are unique and would only be understood by people like them. They see themselves as too good for the ordinary or average, associating only with high-status things, places, and people.

This sense of self also translates into the way these people expect to be treated. They will expect to be recognized without earning such recognition with their talents and achievements. They talk about their relationships and work in terms of their greatness and how much their contribution is. They appear to be saying that other people are lucky to have them as they are the undisputed and only star. Everyone else is only a player, at best.

- *Living in a fantasy world supporting their delusions*

When reality fails to support their delusions of grandeur, narcissists resort to a fantasy world that is propped up by magical thinking, distortion, and self-deception. They spin fantasies to self-glorify, casting themselves as powerful, successful, brilliant, attractive, and ideal. These fantasies will help to protect narcissists from inner feelings of shame and emptiness. They allow them to ignore and rationalize away opinions and facts that contradict them. Anything that threatens to burst their bubble is met with rage and defensiveness. Narcissists deny reality.

- *Need for constant admiration and praise*

The sense of superiority in the narcissist is like a balloon. It loses air without a steady stream of recognition and applause. An occasional compliment does not meet the threshold. Narcissists need to have their ego fed continuously, and so they hang around people who will cater to their obsessive cravings for affirmation. They tend to have one-sided relationships, which are all about what the admirer can do for the narcissist. It is never about the other person's needs. If the praise and attention from the admirer ever diminishes, the narcissist feels betrayed.

- *A sense of entitlement*

Since narcissists imagine they are unique, they expect favors. They believe that they should get anything they want. They expect people around them to oblige their every whim and wish. If you fail to anticipate and meet any need they have, you become useless. You get outrage or the cold shoulder for having the nerve to defy their will.

- *Exploiting other people without shame or guilt*

Narcissists do not know how to identify other people's feelings. They have not learned how to see other people's perspectives. Their lack of empathy comes from the fact that they see people as live objects, existing to serve their needs.

Consequently, they do not hesitate to take advantage of other people to achieve their goals. Sometimes this exploitation is malicious, and other times it is oblivious. Narcissists will not think about the effects of their behavior on other people. Even if you try telling them, they still only understand their needs.

- *Intimidating, demeaning, bullying and belittling other people*

Narcissists get intimidated by meeting people with something they do not have – especially people who are famous and confident. They also get scared by people who challenge them or who do not kowtow to them. For them, contempt is a defense mechanism. It is the only way they can neutralize a threat and prop their ego up. They excel in putting people down. They also tend to become dismissive and condescending to show the other person how little they mean. They may even bully and insult the other person.

Causes, risk factors, complications and prevention
Scientists do not yet agree on the causes of narcissistic personality disorder. However, they agree that it is likely as complex as other mental health disorders. There is a suspected link to the environment, genetics, and neurobiology. On the environment, the suspicion is that mismatches in parent-child relationships that had excessive criticism or excessive adoration that were poorly attuned to the experiences of the child could cause narcissistic behavior. Children could also inherit some characteristics or develop the traits from their thinking and behavioral patterns.

Narcissistic personality disorder typically affects more males than it does females and starts in early adulthood. However, some children may begin showing traits of narcissism without ever developing the disorder.

The disorder likely affects relationships, causes problems at school or work, causes problems with physical health, and may cause depression, anxiety, and suicidal thoughts. Since the cause of the personality disorder is unknown, preventing the condition may be difficult. However, one can participate in therapy to help them communicate better and cope with emotional distress and conflict better.

Machiavellianism

In 'The Prince,' Niccolo Machiavelli (1527) wrote that 'a wise ruler should never keep faith when in so doing it goes against his interests,' and 'a prince should never lack good reasons when breaking his promise.' According to the philosopher, all virtues, including honesty, are expendable if treachery, deceit, and force are more expedient. In short, influential people should choose Machiavellianism even if that is not their style of leadership.

As a psychological term, Machiavellianism is a personality type that will not choose to be that way but is. They are master manipulators. They do not need to read the book to acquire the knack for duplicity. Temperamentally, their predisposition is to be deceptive, calculating, and conniving. These people are amoral, using others as stepping stones toward a goal. From their point of view, if we allow ourselves to be used, we deserve it.

Everyone can be duplicitous sometimes, depending on the circumstance and the need. For example, if you call in sick when you are not, or you lie to your spouse about your activity, you have the human capacity to lie to others, but not necessarily, this personality disorder. If you feel guilty, such episodes do not reflect your standard behavior.

For the Machiavellian, this behavior is routine.

These people thrive in social situations where boundaries and rules are ambiguous. They can detach from situations emotionally, taking on a cynical outlook to life that allows them to control their impulses and be patient opportunists. They use tactics like friendliness, charm, self-disclosure, pressure, and guilt. Using self-disclosure will enable them to mask their true intentions and to have a basis for plausible deniability if they are detected.

Signs and symptoms
- *A cold and calculating view of other people*

The Machiavellian is strategic. They are willing to cheat, lie, and deceive others to achieve their goals. They are not usually emotionally attached, so there is little that will hold them back from hurting other people. Their views and attitudes are problematic and aversive because they experience emotion shallowly.

- *A lack of hot empathy*

There is a distinction between empathy that is 'cold' and cognitive and emotional empathy, or 'hot' empathy. Cold empathy is where you understand how others think and how they may act in different situations. One may even understand how events unfold involving specific people. For instance, a manager might use cold empathy to understand the actions that occur when they give an employee negative feedback to have them display defensiveness. The same manager could also recruit hot empathy to connect with an employee emotionally. For instance, knowing that the feedback would embarrass them, they want to give it constructively. In the second example, the manager is careful not to harm their employee emotionally.

A Machiavellian manager may understand how their employee would react and yet fail to resonate with them emotionally. The result would be that the manager comes across as unfriendly and harsh. They may even fail to realize the emotional harm they have caused.

- *Duplicity*

Duplicity is about a contradictory doubleness of thought, action, or speech. The Machiavellian will hide their true intentions, continually saying one thing and doing another. Note that self-care is not to be confused with this trait unless when it goes overboard. An important fact to note is that these people are tactical. They reveal information for specific reasons that give them an advantage. People in relationships with them will always feel like they are missing a puzzle piece. Even when proper information is provided, there is a reason. They never tell something just for the sake of you knowing it.

Psychopathy

People with this personality disorder lack empathy and other emotions. This lack of emotions allows them to manipulate other people. This trait also makes it difficult to spot a psychopath. They appear healthy and charming, but they have no conscience within. They tend to be antisocial, which makes them inclined to criminality.

Psychopaths have become a popular fascination for clinical study, with professionals finding their patients impervious to treatment. In everyday talk, you will hear psychopathy used interchangeably with sociopathy and often, to refer to people with antisocial tendencies. However, the two are quite different. Psychopathic tendencies are innate and often common for people with chaotic or violent upbringings. Other people think the differences between the two lie in the severity of the symptoms.

Brain anatomy, the environment of the person, and genetics will support the development of these traits. Unlike the other two in the dark triad, psychopathy is a spectrum disorder, diagnosable using different checklists, depending on the clinical institution. However, all checklists check for empathy, pathological lying, and impulsivity.

Psychopaths will display most of the following characteristics:
- Superficial charm
- Need for unending stimulation
- Manipulation
- Pathological lying
- A lack of remorse
- Promiscuous sexual behavior
- Parasitic lifestyles
- Reduced emotional responses
- Grandiose sense of self-worth
- Lack of realistic, long-term goals
- Impulsivity

It is important to remember that the term psychopath is not an official diagnosis. Experts will often classify the signs under ASPD.

The dark side of human consciousness: theories

So far, the focus has been on phenomena as it is observed from outside. In this section, the job is to explain what is happening inside of the mind when someone acts as they do.

Evolutionary advantage

One theory explains the behavior of Machiavellians as an evolutionary advantage. Research on different Machiavellians has shown that some can understand feelings and emotions, except they do not care. One subgroup of Machiavellians has been found to 'bypass empathy.' These people understand the feelings and thoughts that may arise in others as a result of manipulation and deceit or any other form of ill-treatment, but they do nothing to change their actions.

Evolutionary psychologists explain this lack of a moral conscience as evolutionarily advantageous in that the individual will not be held back by considering others as they pursue their goal. The question then becomes how such people can maintain long-lasting relationships that are emotionally satisfying if they cannot show concern for the feelings of others.

Theory of mind

Theory of mind refers to the Machiavellian ability to understand and appreciate why people do things the way that they choose to. The theory of mind is different from empathy. It refers to aspirations, goals, contents, and the desires contained within someone's mind instead of moment-to-moment changes in feeling and thinking.

Theoretically speaking, Machiavellians have a reasonably good theory of mind to get what drives other people to manipulate them. According to research, the theory of mind must also be supported by cooperative social skills. This means that the Machiavellian may be looking to manipulate others but it is not always guaranteed that their manipulation will be successful.

Behavioral inhibition

This theory suggests that behavior is driven by two neurological systems: the behavioral inhibition system and the behavioral activation system. The activation system is concerned with the 'approach' and controls social behavior and extraversion. The inhibition system is concerned with thinking instead of doing and is responsible for tendencies like introversion and withdrawn behavior.

According to recent evidence, narcissism and psychopathy are associated with high activity levels in the activation system, while Machiavellianism is associated with more significant activity in the inhibition system. Going by this theory, narcissists and psychopaths will likely engage in behavior like socializing, while Machiavellians will probably withdraw and rely on intuition and thinking. This evidence is consistent with the profile of Machiavellians as calculating and cunning manipulators who work against others without violating their rights as psychopaths do.

Alexithymia

Alexithymia is a term used to describe a deficit in understanding and naming one's emotions. This is a common explanation for Machiavellianism. People with alexithymia are cold and aloof. They tend to be out of touch with their emotional experiences. In Machiavellianism, this condition may be a result of a low understanding of emotions that comes from shallowly experiencing those emotions or a deficit in empathy and theory of mind. Regardless, Machiavellians use an overly cognitive approach toward others and themselves.

The Jungian model of the psyche

Few people have influenced modern psychology the way Carl Jung did. He formulated the introversion and extraversion archetypes, the collective unconsciousness, and the modern dream analysis. He coined terms including synchronicity, the complex, and the archetype, and his work formed the basis of the Myers-Briggs Type Indicator, which is a famous personality test staple today.

Among his important works is an in-depth analysis of the psyche that he sums up as 'I understand by the psyche the completeness of all psychic processes, unconscious and conscious.' He separates the psyche from the conventional concept of the mind that limits explanations to the processes in the conscious brain.

According to this model, the psyche is self-regulating. It works like the body where one tries to balance between opposing qualities while at the same time trying to grow in what is called 'individuation.' Jung described the psyche as something that could be divided into parts with archetypes and complexes that are personified and work like secondary selves that together make the whole. The concept of the psyche is broken down into:

The ego

The ego is the center of the field of consciousness. It is the part of the psyche where the consciousness stays, and the sense of existence and identity is found. This part may be seen as a command headquarters that organizes one's intuition, senses, feelings, and thoughts. It regulates access to memory and links the inner and outer worlds. It is how one relates to the external.

How an individual will interact with the outer world is determined by how introverted or extroverted they are and how they use sensation, intuition, feeling, and thinking. Some people interact with the world using one or two of the facets.

The ego forms an archetype of the self during early development as the brain struggles to add value and meaning to various experiences. It is the part of the self that selects the information that is most relevant from the environment and determines how to behave based on that. The rest of the information sinks into the unconscious and may show up later in dreams and visions.

The unconscious

The unconscious comes from an interaction between one's personal growth and the collective unconscious. The content of the unconscious is all things one knows, but they are not actively thinking about, everything that was once conscious but is now forgotten, everything perceived by the senses but not the conscious mind and all things that one feels, remembers, wants and does, involuntarily. It also includes the unintentional repressions of feelings and painful thoughts.

Complexes

Complexes are organizations in the unconscious mind that center around perceptions, wishes, emotions, memories, and patterns formed by experience and by how the person reacts to that experience. By this model, complexes are diverse and roll in automatically, making the person feel like their behavior is out of their control. For example, mentally ill people, or those who are mislabeled as 'possessed,' will have complexes that take over markedly and regularly.

Complexes will be influenced by the collective unconscious and tend to have archetypal elements. For a healthy person, complexes will not be a problem and maybe crucial to balancing views of the ego to allow development. For the mentally unwell, who cannot regulate himself, complexes become overt. The ego is damaged and weak, so it cannot use complexes to self-reflect.

The collective unconscious

The theory here is that the nature of an individual is present from birth and that the environment only brings that out instead of creating it. According to Jung, everyone is born with a blueprint that determines how their lives unfold. The current support for the theory is with animals that go to environments that activate certain behaviors.

By this theory, an archetype is not an inherited idea, but an inherited mode of functioning that corresponds to the way a chick emerges from its egg or a bird its nest, or the way eels will find their way to the Bermuda. The pattern of behavior is biological.

To Jung, these blueprints will be influenced by different archetypes like relatives, significant events, parents, and culture, which come together to find expression in the psyche.

The self

The self is the total of the psyche with its full potential. It is the part that will look forward to wholeness and fulfillment. It drives individuation and the quest for one to reach their fullest potential.

Persona

The persona is the element of personality arising to adapt and serve convenience. It is the masks one has to wear in certain situations – a side of you for work, or family. Otherwise put, the persona is 'public relations' and is the part of the ego that allows social interactions with ease.

People who identify with their personas strongly run into problems. Here, consider a celebrity to becomes too involved with themselves as a 'star' that they carry work everywhere or the academic who looks down on everyone. An attachment to the persona can stunt growth as it grows from a desire to please parents, teachers, and authority figures. It leans toward embodying the best qualities and leaving out the negative ones that contradict the persona, forming a shadow.

The shadow

The traits that you prefer to ignore or dislike form the shadow. It is the part of the psyche influenced by the collective unconscious and is a form of complex, except it is accessible to the conscious mind.

The shadow is seen as a must-have because 'where there is light, there has to be a shadow.' It balances the psyche. If it is not well developed, a person can become shallow and preoccupied with the opinions of other people. The way conflict helps to advance the plot of a novel; the shadow is vital for personal growth.

People who would rather not face their shadow side project onto others, explaining the idea that the qualities one is unable to stand in others, one has, but does not see them. Growth requires casting aside the willful blindness and trying to balance the persona.

Anima and animus

Anima and animus are contra-sexual psyche archetypes. Anima is in the man and animus in the woman. The two come from masculine and feminine archetypes that the individual experiences in their interactions with the opposite sex, starting with the parent. Like the shadow, they work to balance out a possibly one-sided gender experience. One then starts to look for a reflection of their animus or anima in a mate, explaining the idea of 'love at first sight.' Jung defines masculinity and femininity as two sides of a coin, or two halves of a whole.

Individuation

Individuation is the quest for wholeness that the psyche invariably undertakes. It is the journey to becoming conscious of oneself as a unique person in the same sense that all people are. According to the model, conflict is inherent to human psychology and even necessary for growth. In dealing with challenges, one becomes creative, conscious, and enlightened.

Connecting the theories and dark psychology

Whether or not you are aware of it, psychological models govern your everyday behavior. Dark psychology only studies the way people prey upon others. However, even for the victim, there are behavior patterns that cause them to be as they are.

Note that all humanity has the potential to victimize other humans. What makes the difference is knowing when to sublimate or restrain the tendency and how to interact with people who act on impulses, without awareness. Dark psychology is about understanding the feelings, thoughts, and perceptions behind predatory behavior. It assumes a goal-oriented and rational purpose most of the time.

To fully grasp the concept, one needs to remember the following:

- *Dark psychology is universal and integrally part of the human condition.*

It is a construct that has exerted influence throughout cultures, societies, and people all through history. The most benevolent people have known about it but refuse to act upon it. They have lower rates of violent feelings and thoughts.

- *It is the study of people's feelings, thoughts, and perceptions in relation to an innate potential to prey on others without apparent reasons.*

All behavior is goal-oriented, conceptualized, and purposive, but dark psychology suggests that the closer a person gets to the 'black hole' of pure evil, the less likely they will have a purpose in their motivations. It assumes that some people are close to pristine evil.

- *It is easy to overlook in its latent form as it may be misinterpreted as aberrant psychopathy.*

History is filled with examples of this tendency, revealing itself as destructive and active behaviors. Modern psychology and psychiatry call a psychopath a predator, lacking in remorse for his actions. This science states that there is a severity continuum with feelings and thoughts of violence to extreme violence and victimization without reasonable motivation.

Types of mind control

Stories have been told through movies and by the media about groups of people who were hypnotized or brainwashed into doing things they would not otherwise do. When such stories emerge, people jump to both sides of the issue. Some deny the existence of mind control, while others start to believe that they could be mind-controlled at any moment.

Conspiracy theories spring up about government officials and people in power. Even some courts accept 'brainwashing' as an explanation for people committing the crimes they have been accused of.

This section explores dark psychology at work in real life. It looks to explain the fascination and fear people have had with the ideas of mind control and being forced to do things against their will.

Brainwashing

Brainwashing is the process where someone is convinced to leave the beliefs they had in the past to adopt new ideas and values. There are many ways that this is achieved. The underlying idea is to manipulate human action or thought against the will, desire, and knowledge of the individual.

In controlling the physical and social environment, one aims to destroy the loyalties that are unfavorable to specific individuals or groups. The victim must then admit that their attitudes and patterns are incorrect and then change them. They then need to develop unquestioning obedience and loyalty to the ruling party.

Brainwashing is mostly used to refer to religious or political indoctrination and ideological remolding. Brainwashing techniques will involve isolating from former sources of information and associates, a strict regimen needing absolute humility and obedience, strong social pressures and rewards when one co-operates and punishments – physical or psychological – for non-cooperation. Those who do not conform could become ostracized and criticized, derived of sleep or food, and tortured by their social contacts.

Communist political prisons in China, 1949, were the first reports of brainwashing. The practice continued after the Vietnamese and Korean wars. Nowadays, there are reports of the use of brainwashing by radical political groups and religious cults.

After brainwashing, one has to deprogram to reverse the effects. They have to confront the beliefs that they have come to embrace through psychotherapy.

There are other methods of brainwashing that are not frowned upon. For example, moving to a new place may need you to adjust your ideals and values to fit into the new surroundings and culture.

During brainwashing, the subject is separated from the things they know. They are broken down emotionally until they become emotionally vulnerable, and then new concepts are introduced. As the subject absorbs the new information they are receiving, they get social rewards.

Another example of brainwashing happens online. Before social media, people interacted with TV advertisements and other advertising on newspapers and billboards. Such advertisements would only appeal to people interested in a specific product. Social media has made it that advertising is personalized. Platforms are committed to displaying relevant advertisements based on the information you provide.

However, since the information one provides allows the creation of a psychological profile, one is soon introduced to things they do not want and convinced over time that they need those to survive, and hence a new frontier into brainwashing and yet using the same principles.

Hypnosis

During hypnosis, the hypnotist has to put you in a trance-like state to focus your concentration. The hypnotist uses mental images and repetition to break through psychological barriers and allow you to buy into some ideas.

During hypnotherapy, the therapist might help you gain control over undesired behaviors that you have or to cope with pain and anxiety. For a long time, hypnosis was associated with sideshow performances before it got its way into the clinical field.

Hypnotherapy could prove useful for:

- **Pain control** – Hypnosis can help patients suffering from cancer, fibromyalgia, irritable bowel syndrome, and temporomandibular joint problems. It is used in childbirth and dental procedures.
- **Hot flashes** – Hypnosis can help relieve hot flashes that come during menopause.
- **Controlling side effects** – for cancer patients undergoing chemotherapy, hypnotherapy can help ease the side effects.
- **Mental health conditions** – hypnosis can help to treat phobias, anxiety, and post-traumatic stress.
- **Behavior change** – Hypnosis has been used to treat smoking, bed-wetting, overeating, and insomnia.

Manipulation

Manipulation is often used to determine how a person will think. Psychological manipulation borrows from the theories of dark psychology. It is a type of influence exerted to change other people's perceptions. The manipulator will use underhanded, abusive, and deceptive tactics to advance their interests, often at the expense of others.

Most people recognize manipulation at work but fail to identify it as a form of mind control. It is particularly evasive to pin if the manipulator is someone well known to you. A lighthouse feature of manipulation is where the subject remains feeling as if they do not have a choice in a matter. They might receive half-truths or outright lies and not realize how bad a situation is until it is too late.

If the subject finds out about the situation ahead of time, the agent may use it to blackmail them. Essentially, the subject is stuck because the agent crafts everything so that they get into no trouble. The subject has to accept blame for the situation, and the agent has achieved their final goal.

The hardest part about manipulation for the subject is that the agent cannot feel their needs, and neither do they care who gets harmed in the process. Meanwhile, the agent can walk away unscathed because they were not emotionally invested in the situation. If the manipulator is an expert, they can turn things around quickly to make the subject feel like they are crazy.

Chapter 2: Understanding Manipulation

In the romantic comedy films, the main characters find a way to end up together. They jump through the obstacles and fight day and night to keep their love alive. Off-screen, however, love is not always enough to make any relationship last.

Feelings of romantic love, which are often intense, can convince people to keep fighting for an unhealthy and unfulfilling relationship that leaves them unhappy. For example, people looking at images of their partner cause dopamine to be released in the body, which is responsible for making someone feel good.

Feel-good chemicals cause people to overlook logical choices, like leaving unsatisfying relationships. Endorphins drive people in love. While such chemicals will make you feel good, those feelings alone will not make the connection stable and lasting.

Often, people will wonder when to know that they should leave a relationship. If your needs are not being met, it may be an indication that you need to go. In this case, needs include emotional needs like wanting quality time with your partner, or even financial.

For most people, it is easy to recognize situations where their needs are not being met. However, it becomes more complicated if there is manipulation involved. The first sign of manipulation in a casual encounter or close relationship is often a feeling of being controlled or pressured. You will likely also begin to question yourself more than you usually do.

Manipulation is a psychological strategy typically used by emotionally unhealthy people who are incapable of directly asking for what they want or need. These people, knowingly or not, end up trying to control others to get their needs met.

There are different types of manipulation, ranging from an abusive partner to a pushy salesperson. Some behaviors are easier to spot than others.

It is important to note that regardless of the context, manipulation is about exercising undue influence through emotional exploitation and mental distortion. The intention is usually to seize control, power, and get privileges at the expense of the victim.

It is also critical to note the difference between healthy social influence and psychological manipulation. A healthy social influence happens between two people and is part of constructive and meaningful relationships. In psychological relationships, one person is used to benefit the other. The manipulator creates a power imbalance and uses it to exploit the victim to serve their agenda.

Most people will manipulate others periodically. For example, if you tell your friend that you feel 'fine' when you are depressed, that is technically a way to manipulate because you control their perceptions of you and how they react to you.

The consequences of manipulation can be insidious. They are made especially so because they are associated with emotional abuse within the context of intimate relationships. As such, manipulation will affect a person's mental health.

In everyday situations, people manipulate from deep-seated anxiety or fear. The manipulator is unable to connect with their authentic self while the manipulated becomes emotionally damaged. Left unaddressed, manipulation could traumatize the victim, especially if they are made to feel ashamed or guilty. They may develop anxiety, fall into depression, lie about their feelings, and develop unhealthy coping mechanisms that further exacerbate the situation. The manipulated may also begin to put the other person's needs above their own, always try to please them and then develop trust issues with other people.

In extreme cases, the manipulated could begin questioning their perceptions of reality. In the movie Gaslight, the husband subtly manipulates the wife until she stops trusting her opinions. In one scene, the husband covertly turns down the gaslights and convinces her that the dimming lights were just in her head.

Manipulation and mental health

While most people will manipulate others from time to time, those who have a chronic pattern of manipulation may be suffering from an underlying medical health concern.

People with personality disorder diagnoses such as narcissistic personality (NPD) or borderline personality (BPD) are prone to manipulating others. For BPD, manipulation will mean meeting their emotional needs or validating them when they are feeling abandoned or insecure. Many people learn to turn to manipulation after experiencing abuse. It becomes, for them, a coping mechanism to get their needs indirectly met.

Narcissists, on the other hand, manipulate for different reasons. They have a hard time forming close relationships, and so manipulation helps to 'keep' their partner in the relationship. They will continuously shame the other party, play victim, or gaslight their partner to gain affection or attention.

In close relationships, even between friends and family members, manipulation can deteriorate the health of a relationship, causing poor mental health and sometimes the dissolution of the said relationship.

In a marriage or a domestic partnership, manipulation will have one partner feeling worthless, isolated, and bullied. In healthy relationships, people may inadvertently manipulate others as they try to avoid confrontation, or as they try not to burden their partners.

There are numerous cases of people who know when they are being manipulated but choose to downplay the situation or overlook it. In intimate relationships, manipulation can take forms like guilt, exaggeration, keeping secrets, passive aggression, gift-giving, and showing affection selectively.

Manipulation may also exist between parent-child relationships. The parent ends up setting up the child for anxiety, depression, and other mental health conditions. Studies show that parents who regularly manipulate their children increase the likelihood of the children using manipulation to get their needs met. Such parents will likely downplay the achievements of the child, withhold affection, and make the child feel guilty for their desires.

People will also feel manipulated in friendships that become toxic. In such friendships, one person may be meeting their own needs at the expense of their friend. A manipulative friend will use coercion or guilt to extract favors like reaching out only when they need their emotional needs met or loaning money, or even finding excuses when the friend needs the relationship.

The motives behind manipulation vary from malicious to unconscious. The first chapter of the book discussed what is happening in the mind of the manipulator. In the next section, you will understand ways to identify when you are on the receiving end of manipulation. The idea is to help you break out of such circumstances and watch out for your safety and interests.

Psychological signs of manipulation

- *You feel fear, guilt, and obligation*

Manipulation involves guilt, obligation, and fear. When someone is manipulating you, they psychologically coerce you into doing something you do not want to do. You might feel obligated or scared to do it, or you might feel guilty if you do not do it.

There are two common types of manipulators – the 'victim' and the 'bully.' The bully will make you fearful and may use threats, intimidation, and aggression to control you. The victim causes the target to feel guilt. They act 'hurt' while they create the problem, in reality.

The person targeted by the manipulator playing victim will often try to help the manipulator so that they stop feeling guilty. Such targets will feel responsible for assisting the victim by doing whatever is necessary to alleviate their suffering.

- *You are questioning yourself*

Gaslighting is a term used to identify manipulation where the manipulated begins to question their thoughts, memory, and reality. A manipulative person will twist what you say and will make it about them. They will hijack the conversation to make you feel like you are in the wrong when you cannot see anything you have done wrong.

A person being gaslighted may feel a false sense of defensiveness or guilt. You feel like you have failed to do something when that is not the case. Manipulators will not take responsibility for their actions.

- *There are strings attached*

In manipulation, people will not do you a favor because it is fun and free. There will be strings attached. Every good thing done will have an expectation that will have you made out to be ungrateful. The manipulator will exploit the expectations and norms of reciprocity.

A salesperson could, for example, make it appear as if they gave you a deal, and because they did, you should buy the product. In a relationship, a partner could buy you flowers and ask you to return the favor. These tactics will usually work because they abuse norms. Reciprocating favors is normal, but one will often feel a need to comply and reciprocate even when it is done insincerely.

- *'Door-in-the face' and 'Foot-in-the-door' techniques*

In the foot-in-the-door technique, the manipulator starts with a small and reasonable request. They might ask if you, for example, have time. The request opens the door for a more significant request, which keeps escalating until you are unable to say no. Most street scams will use this technique.

The 'door-in-the-face' technique involves someone starting with a big request. When the request is rejected, they make a smaller one and keep going until they get the request they wanted in the first place. For instance, someone doing contract work could ask for a large sum of money upfront. After declining, they keep negotiating for smaller amounts, and the logic is that a smaller amount will have a more considerable appeal in comparison to the larger amount.

- *Your needs are not being met*

Every person has needs they require met in a relationship. When one partner is not fulfilling these requirements, the neglected partner must communicate. If the demands are not met, it is best that the partner move on. In a manipulative relationship, the victim will have no sense of self to leave the relationship. They become convinced that they will not find anyone better than their partner. Eventually, they become addicted to the intermittent reinforcement they get from being in the relationship and perpetuate their unhappiness.

- *You are seeking out others to meet your needs*

When you get promoted at work or when you receive good news, who is it that you want to tell the good news? In a healthy and fulfilling relationship, you should want to tell your partner. There is trust and support to help you through even the hard seasons of life. If, when presented with the choice to inform your boyfriend or your guy friend something you turn to your guy friend, it may be an indication that you are not getting the emotional affirmation you need. Seeking physical and emotional fulfillment from outside your relationship may be an indication that it is time to end that relationship. Note that this factor alone does not point to manipulation, but should be assessed alongside other factors.

- *You are afraid to ask more from your partner*

Naturally, there is discomfort in bringing up a need that your partner is not meeting in your relationship. However, if the lines of communication are not open, it may be a sign that there is emotional dysfunction. If you find yourself afraid of sounding emotional or needy, preferring instead to suppress how you feel, there might be a problem. You may be in a manipulative relationship if you have to feign contentment for fear of feeling like you are a burden. In situations like this, there is likely to happen something that will break the camel's back, and the argument that follows ends up damaging the relationship.

An unaddressed issue or a single case of manipulation that goes unacknowledged grows into more manipulation. Before long, the victim also feels a need to manipulate by hiding their true feelings from their partner.

- *Your loved ones disapprove of the relationship*

In some cases, you may be in deep with your partner until you do not recognize manipulation as it happens. It is always a good idea to take account of what your trusted family members and friends think about your relationship. If the community around you refuses to support you, it may be a red flag. People close to you can see if the person you are with is not making you happy. As manipulation progresses, you may find that you are beginning to lie to your friends and yourself. Further interactions with the said partner cause you to withdraw so that you do not have to listen to what your loved ones have to say.

Tricks manipulators use

- *Home court advantage*

Here, the manipulative person insists on your meeting and interacting in a physical space. The point here is for them to be able to exert more control and dominance. The physical space is often the manipulator's home, car, office, or area where they feel familiar or ownership.

- *Letting you speak first to find your baseline and weaknesses*

Many salespeople will use this tactic. They prospect you by asking general and yet probing questions. The idea is for them to create a baseline about your behavior and thinking. From that, they can evaluate your strengths and weaknesses. This type of questioning often has a hidden agenda. It can be found in workplace relationships and friendships, as well.

- *Manipulating facts*

Here, the manipulator will twist the facts to suit their ends. Manipulation of facts can come in the form of lying, making excuses, or being two-faced. Victim blaming is also another form of manipulating facts. Deforming the truth, withholding critical information, exaggerating, understating, and strategic disclosure are forms of manipulation.

- *Overwhelming you with statistics and facts*

Some people enjoy 'intellectual bullying.' Here, the manipulator presumes to be the most knowledgeable in some areas. They take advantage of you by exposing you to statistics, facts, and alleged data that you do not know. This often happens in financial and sales situations or other professional negotiations and discussions. However, some people use the same technique in relational arguments. By presuming a power, they exert over you, the manipulator hopes to push through their agenda more convincingly. Other people use this technique to feel a sense of intellectual superiority.

- *Overwhelming you with red tape and procedures*

Some people will use bureaucracy – procedures, laws, paperwork, by-laws, and committees to maintain a position of power while making your life difficult. This technique is used as a delay tactic to keep truth-seeking at bay and hide weaknesses, flaws, and evade scrutiny.

- *Displaying negative emotions and raising their voice*

Some people raise their voices in conversations as a form of manipulation. The assumption for them is that if they project loudly enough, or if they display negative emotions, you submit to their demands and capitulate. The aggressive voice will often be accompanied by strong body language like excited gestures and upright posture to increase impact.

- *Negative surprises*

Other people use negative surprises to off-balance you and gain an advantage over you. The surprises can range from low balling in a situation where you are negotiating to a profession that they will be unable to deliver in one way. The negative information will often come up without warning, and so you will have no time to prepare to counter the move. The manipulator may ask you to concede further so that they keep working with you.

- *Giving you no time to decide*

This tactic is popular with salespeople. The manipulator will pressure you to decide before you are ready for it. By applying tension and control, they hope that you 'crack' and meet their demands.

- *Cynical humor that pokes at your weaknesses and disempowers*

Some manipulators will make critical remarks and disguise them as sarcasm or humor to make you seem less secure or inferior. For example, one such person could comment on your appearance. Comments could even touch on the model of your phone, your credentials, and even your background. Anything, including your walking in late and out of breath, is fair game. By making you look bad and feel bad, the manipulator hopes to gain psychological superiority.

- *Consistently criticizing or judging you to make you feel inadequate*

Different from the previous tactic where the manipulator uses humor as cover, here, the manipulator will pick on you out rightly. They will continuously marginalize you, dismiss you, or ridicule you to keep you off balance and maintain superiority. The aggressor will deliberately foster the impression that there is something amiss with you and that regardless of how you try, you are inadequate. They make you feel like you are not good enough. Significantly, the manipulator may also zoom in on the negative without offering constructive solutions or offering genuine ways to help.

- *Silent treatment*

The manipulator deliberately fails to respond to your reasonable text messages, emails, calls, and other inquiry. They assume power by making you wait. They intend to place uncertainty and doubt in your mind. The silent treatment is often used as a leverage form.

- *Pretend ignorance*

With pretend ignorance, the manipulator 'plays dumb.' They pretend that they do not understand what you want or what you expect of them. They passive-aggressively make you take on what is their job. Some children will use this tactic to stall or manipulate adults into performing tasks they do not want to do. Some grown-ups also use this tactic when they have a duty they would like to avoid or something to hide.

- *Guilt-baiting*

In this case, the manipulator will blame their victim unreasonably. They target the recipient's soft spot and hold them responsible for their success, happiness, or their failures and unhappiness. By targeting the emotional weakness and the vulnerability of the victim, the manipulator coerces the recipient into meeting unreasonable demands and requests.

- *Victimhood*

Sometimes the manipulator will use imagined or exaggerated personal issues to exert control. They might use co-dependency, powerlessness, martyrdom, or even deliberate frailty in a bid to elicit favor and sympathy from their victim. The purpose of this victimhood is to exploit the goodwill of the recipient, their sense of obligation, their protective instinct, or their good conscience to extract unreasonable concessions and benefits.

Dealing with manipulative people

How you respond to manipulation depends on the type of manipulation you face. If you think someone is manipulating you, or even being abusive, it is best to find help breaking the assumption that the behavior is normal. Often, and subconsciously, you begin to believe that manipulation is normal.

In other cases, the simple solution might be not to take manipulative behavior personally. 'Observe, don't absorb' is an excellent mantra to live by. That way, you are not responsible for other people's feelings.

Be sure to establish boundaries to keep manipulation at bay. Manipulators tend to have bad boundaries. They either have boundaries that are enmeshed or too rigid. If you catch yourself in a manipulative situation, it may be useful to delay your response. Avoid making major decisions in a manipulative situation; otherwise, you regret the choice.

When it becomes toxic, dealing with other people's behavior becomes exhausting.

At the workplace, manipulation can reduce performance and make for a toxic workplace. If you feel manipulated in any situation, consider the following:

- *Disengage*

When a person is trying to get a specific emotional response from you, do not give it to them. For instance, if a manipulative friend flatters you before asking for a favor, refuse to play along. Instead, politely move the conversation to other things.

- *Be confident*

In other cases, manipulation works because the manipulator causes you to doubt your abilities, reality, and intuition. When this happens, stick to your story. If this occurs in the context of a close relationship, it is best to leave it.

- *Address the issue*

Be vigilant to call out manipulative behavior while it is happening. Focus on the way a person's actions are affecting you instead of accusing them. That way, there are higher chances of reaching a resolution while being careful to draw boundaries.

- *Keep to the topic*

After pointing out behavior that makes you feel manipulated, the other person will likely muddle the situation or try to minimize it by bringing other issues up to distract you. Remain by your point and stick to it.

It might be a good idea to seek out therapy if you have been in manipulative relationships for an extended period. In therapy, you get to address the underlying issues.

For instance, someone whose manipulative behavior is caused by underlying mental issues may benefit from individual therapy to understand how unhealthy their behavior is, for themselves and others. A counselor could also help a manipulative person learn life skills to use as they interact with people, respecting boundaries, and addressing any underlying insecurities that may cause the behavior.

Chapter 3: Master the art of persuasion

Persuasion is the act of winning someone over to your beliefs or having them do something you suggest. It has often been called an art, but one wonders why that is as-is and what it means.

This chapter concentrates on unpacking the term, explaining the principles, and suggesting ways to become more persuasive. The idea is to help you learn how to persuade others. It will also help you to be more aware when other people work to convince you.

Persuasion is an integral part of life and society. No wonder the psychology of persuasion is interesting because one also has to study different aspects of life and different contexts as they unfold. The psychology of persuasion is, therefore, a broad study.

By definition, persuasion is a process of communication to try and convince people to change their attitudes and even behavior regarding an issue by transmitting a message in an atmosphere of free choice. Persuasion differs from manipulation in that the recipient of the communication has free choice and few to no consequences of failing to oblige. Substantially, persuasion is influencing other people in a free choice society through:

- Sounds, images, and words
- Deliberate attempts to influence others
- Focusing on the free choice of the people
- Media, either non-verbally or verbally.

How persuasion has changed with time

People have been persuading each other to do things since the beginning of time. In the past, however, some elements that were seen as persuasion were not. Persuasion may include manipulation, which causes many people to find it distasteful. It is mainly so when the actual intent behind persuasion is social control. If you have no interest or power, then you are not considered influential. Consequently, one school of thought thinks persuasion to be a bad type of social control, but an excellent way to communicate a message.

In the liberal arts of the Middle Ages, artists and other educated men had mastered the art of persuasion, using it to become leaders. Preachers used scripture to inspire change and to rally the country together. Tribes persuaded their neighbors to join forces or to trade food. Persuasion even caused wars.

Persuasion is more than influencing people, however. It is used in advertising and informs many of the principles behind it.

Only a hundred years ago, there were not many effective ways to communicate with the populace. Access to the radio and television paved the way to social media and the internet.

As mediums and messages change partly due to the influence of technology, persuasion also changed. Nowadays, it is done on a grander scale to influence more people. It is now like a science. Those who engage do not just want the attention of the target groups, but also to win them over.

Persuasion has become more prominent, faster, subtler, and more complex. It is used by big businesses and is part of their growth and expansion plans. One needs only to look at a television commercial to see how much persuasion there is. The average user interacts with up to ten television advertisements per hour and even more on their phone as they scroll through their social media feed. You become exposed between 300 and 3000 different advertisements and images meant to win you over toward a particular way of thinking, some more compelling than others. Every one of the involved brands wants to communicate and to touch on the right points when they have your attention.

In this internet age, persuasion also happens fast. News of a CEO who has been sucked or a company that has a promotion spreads like a wildfire. Other than advertising companies, marketing firms, and PR agencies also use persuasion. Everyone wants to create social influence.

While persuasion is about influencing the other person, some types of persuasion will deal with the psyche more than others. Some advertisers use subtle ads and images to create a result. Others use images that are different from their message to capture your interest before shifting to their message. In other cases, advertisers use a lifestyle issue, playing at the viewer's lifestyle. Sex has become a primary selling point because many people enjoy it.

In that sense, persuasion is more than telling people what you want them to hear or that you want them to pay attention. One has to create interest. In the past, one could be persuasive using less because there were fewer competitors.

Communication in persuasion

Notably, there can be no persuasion without communication. If you are unable to pass your point effectively, you will not be successful in persuading your hearers.

In communication, you have to get the attention of your audience. They need to be able to comprehend the content of your message for you to be persuasive. In practice, you have to get the person to yield to the point you are fighting for and then gain their interest. If you keep them interested for long enough, they begin to act on your message, and your persuasion is successful.

In other cases, the goal of persuasion is to get a whole group to act. For instance, getting people to believe in Christianity took persuasion.

Some theorists enforce a connection between persuasion and education. Teaching is integral to the communication process and can play a role in winning someone over. Secondly, part of teaching is repetition, which can cause a person to modify their behavior. If you are persuasive, the learner becomes verbally conditioned.

An example of persuasion in real-life conversations is where you talk to someone about their interests. They tell you all the reasons they like the said thing, and through your repeated discussions, you develop an interest in the said thing. Learning emphasizes retention and attention, which are vital to communication.

Researchers agree on the following elements of persuasion:

- *Reciprocity*

What do I get in return if I invest my energy, time, and money in this situation? The basic idea here is that reciprocity is wired in your DNA. When someone does something nice for you, you feel the need to do something nice for them in return.

- *Commitment and consistency*

Consistency helps people to stick around for long enough to commit to something. While most people like to believe in the diversity of life choices, it is also true that most are in their comfort zone. When hounded by choice, one sticks with what they know to be more comfortable, playing to the fear of the unknown. Committing to something can help you convince people. Brands use this principle by asking people to buy something small first and then rewarding loyalty with deals and programs that keep the customer coming back.

- *Social proof*

What evidence is there that what you are selling works? Social proof is about getting the endorsement of experts, large groups, celebrities, or people who use the product. People like getting recommendations from people they already trust. Sometimes, all a marketer needs to do to be persuasive is to get reviews from such people.

- *Liking*

This influences how people work with you. It can be anything from attractiveness to compliments. In the liking principle, you are convinced by someone you like, whether they are loved ones, friends, or family. It can also involve strangers you find attractive who recommend something. Attractiveness is not just confined to physical appearance. It could also cover a user-friendly website or quality images.

- *Authority*

People are more inclined to work with you if you appear like you know what you are doing. Citing research, working with scientists, or even talking with experts, gives the impression of being an authority. One example of this principle is where advertisements use the term 'according to research' or 'science says.' The person buying the product will not wonder what research is referred to; the implication of authority is enough to cause them to gravitate toward the product.

- *Scarcity*

To persuade someone when you have something that is one-of-a-kind or limited is easier. People easily drift toward things for the sake of the rarity. Often, in commercials, you are promised an exclusive offer if you keep watching. Usually, these offers have limited time. The urgency helps to lend the product a sense of exclusivity and gives the customer an incentive to buy the product. Another example of this principle is when in an auction; the auctioneer convinces you that the product is competitive.

These elements help you to get to the point of selling something to another person. They allow you to bypass the rational mind and work with the subconscious. No wonder some people choose brands they do not know to serve their needs. Effective marketing is about reaching out to the psyche.

Often, people interact with the idea of persuasion and imagine themselves exempt from its influences. However, persuasion affects everyone. At times, you can avoid pushy people, but at any one point, saying no to one thing means saying yes to another. Besides, with the subtlety of persuasion now, one may not be aware of how affected they are unless they intentionally take stock.

Persuasion as an art

To understand why and how persuasion is an art, one has to consider the broad definition of art. Philosophically, art is any activity that expresses intense emotion, is intellectually challenging, and is coherent and complex. The messages it communicates have to be shown from an individual point of view, it has to be original, and the performance needs a high degree of skill. Art is also the product of an attempt to produce art.

While not all these things will apply to persuasion, effective persuasion has to embody most of these traits. For instance, a marketer can be persuasive without using emotion, but they have to work at producing an artistic piece of advertising that needs high skill and comes from someone's perspective. Persuasion as an art is not necessarily a published painting or music album. You can persuade without being artistic.

However, persuasion must convey complex messages, must challenge the viewer intellectually and can be original,

What then is the point?

Persuading other people is not about manipulation. Every successful person has had to convince people to join their course at one point or the other. If nothing else, most people, in their lives, will need to convince an employer to hire them.

Salespeople persuade people to buy their services or products. Politicians have to convince voters to vote for them. Con artists have to win their victim over to fall for the scam. Persuasion runs through every human endeavor. You may need to persuade your teacher to give you a makeup test or your boyfriend to marry you. You may need to convince someone to volunteer for a program. It is difficult getting anyone to do anything at all without using a form of persuasion.

Practicing persuasion

Anyone can become persuasive at one point in their lives, but few people do it well. The following are things one can learn from those who have a knack for convincing people to see things their way:

- *Assess difficulty*

Get a feel for how difficult it will be to win your audience over. The following are factors you might want to consider:

If you are a member of a group, it may be challenging to convince the group members to go against the aims and the subjects of the group. Its existence and your loyalty to it strengthen your resolve to stick to their version of the truth.

Self-esteem influences how receptive people are to a message. Those with low self-esteem are easier to convince because they place a higher premium on other people's opinions than their own.

People who do not like to show aggression will much more likely be overtaken by smooth talkers who are persuasive. They often find themselves uncomfortable about situations but failing to resist because they are not prone to displaying aggression and challenging the other person.

People with depressive tendencies will be easier to convince than healthier people.

People who think of themselves as socially inadequate are easier to persuade. Even if they are not socially inept compared to others, their view of self, causes them to lay the burden of conversation on the person they are interacting with. They consequently become easy to convince without challenge.

- *Get the right introduction*

It is harder to go up to a stranger to convince them of something than it is to convince someone you are already acquainted with. No wonder many salespeople do not like cold-calling. In cold calling, you do not know who the person is, what their preferences are, and whether or not they belong to groups you disagree with. The stranger does not recognize you either.

A good rule of thumb is to get an introduction from someone they know. Your chances of persuading them to adopt your viewpoint increase if some rapport is established. If an introduction is not possible, do prep work before trying to convince them of anything.

- *Listen*

In listening first, you can gather the data you need to personalize your pitch to make it sensible to the other person. Savvy political candidates will not just come to your door and begin a lecture. Instead, they ask questions about your perspective to see where to start their persuasion. Additionally, listening makes the other person feel valued and respected, putting them in a favorable position to listen to you.

- *Disagree agreeably*

If you are trying to persuade someone to see your point of view, it is essential to agree with them as often as possible. This shows that you have respect for their opinions. Everyone wants to be considered intelligent, and so refuting all that they say will cause them to ignore you.

Since the point of persuasion is getting them to agree with you, where you do not agree, have an agreeable attitude. Acknowledge their reasoning and affirm the choices that they have made.

- *Be subtle*

If everyone could say precisely what they want and they get their audience to believe them, that would not be persuasion. More often than not, you have to show people the subtle ways that your viewpoint is the best. The most effective techniques for persuasion are not obvious or blatant. They are built from storytelling, drawing comparisons, and meeting someone where they are.

As such, the art of persuasion will require a commitment to the process and patience. If you could ask someone to 'believe you' and they did, there would be no persuasion involved there. Changing people's minds takes time. You have to explain the rationale and develop your arguments consistently. If the message is simple, it does not take long to deliver. If it is complicated, you will require patience.

When you close your arguments, you can present the conclusion as obvious, but people become easier to persuade if they believe themselves to be concluding. They want to buy into your idea and change their actions and viewpoints. If you present a sensible argument, they imagine the conclusion was their idea and will likely hold the opinion and change their behavior.

Ethical concerns about persuasion

There are some ethical dilemmas one has to consider when practicing persuasion. Too many people use the skills they learn maliciously and to take advantage of others. Before you start trying to persuade someone, consider what impact you will have on them if you succeed.

Legally speaking, undue influence is a term used to describe situations where you persuade someone to act against their own free will or without heeding the consequences. It comes into play with incapacitated people who have their ability to make decisions impaired. For instance, when a caregiver convinces an older adult to amend their will to leave them everything, that could be undue influence. If you are considering using persuasion, it is in your moral and legal interests to avoid undue influence.

Another instance when it may get you in trouble with using persuasion is when you falsify evidence. You could be sued for posting on social media, something that is unfair or something that presents falsified images, documents, and statements to prove a point. You want to be considerate and responsible in your practice of persuasion by ensuring that you have evidence to support the information you present.

A final ethical consideration for persuasion is using the art to perpetrate scams. Often, people who scam others do not care whether they hurt others or not. Yet, they will often practice persuasion convincingly. To avoid being involved in scams, get your facts straight, and be on the watch for possible deception.

Like with other arts, persuasion is neither negative nor positive. The goals behind the use determine whether or not you are helping change the world.

Having little ability to persuade others can stand in the way of development in life. You might have trouble buying a home, getting a job, or moving your relationship to the next level. Fortunately, you can learn confidence through persuasion and get the power to present the views you have as viable options.

Conversely, if you find that you are too easily convinced, falling prey to every scam that comes your way, learning persuasion helps you decrease how susceptible you are. Be sure to work on your social skills and self-esteem to become less vulnerable.

Steps to master the art of persuasion

Many entrepreneurs, passionate about their idea, fail to see how an intelligent person, being the customer or investor, would not be excited about it after a short introduction. They fail to realize that they can kill their future opportunities and their credibility by communicating only with passion and responding with sarcastic comments every time a question is asked.

For the entrepreneur, persuasion is having the patience necessary to get people to see things as you see them. You hone it from the first day you formulate an idea. You have to get the right partners to join your cause and to help you be part of the solution. The right investors need to fund it, and you need good marketing to push the whole business forward.

Some principles of dark psychology help win others over even to support your business. The following are pragmatic practices and tactics that have been used by business advisors to get their investments going:

Repetition
It is not enough to assume that your passion will rub off on other people. Passion may make you stand out to one group, but in today's information-overloaded society, you need to repeat your bottom line until you have people's attention. Most people have filters that help them ignore unsolicited inputs until they interact with them verbally or in written form.

Obey the context
Your message needs to be tuned to the situation or context of the receiver. Technical or abstract declarations often sound like an effort to mislead or impress the audience with your intelligence. If you are making a proposal, use specific propositions for value instead of fuzzy terms.

Use contrasts
Stories are often more convincing than statements of fact. If you can involve the receiver in your story, the potential impact is more significant. Pitching two ideas side by side, or contrasting two outcomes is useful in moving people to accept new ideas.

Personalization

If you are looking to persuade investors or customers, for example, you need to know a little about them. That way, you can find a personal intersection of interests with the idea you are selling. A person who is intuitive and creative will respond to the intuitive and innovative ideas and recoil from an analytical or logical message. Be sure to establish a relationship first.

Use connections to make introductions

People are prone to listen to people they already trust and consider new ideas they have to table. Use relationships to introduce you to the people you want to meet. It may take longer to reach them, but you gain impact and credibility that way.

Carry a demo or a prototype

People put more effort into things they can feel or touch versus words and actions. If what you are visualizing is not apparent to the mind, people may find it difficult to get behind you. You are likely to be more successful if you carry a prototype.

Present exciting evidence

If you are looking to be compelling on social media, or to test out your ideas, be sure to pick proof that your audience will be interested in. Social media platforms are excellent places to test out ideas at minimal risks and costs and to amplify your message. When creating content to support your views on social media, use examples that have meaning to the audience. Ideally, you want to see how real people respond to what you are selling outside of a controlled environment.

Principles of persuasion

The basics

Persuasion and manipulation are different. Manipulation will require coercion using force or emotional bullying to get someone to do something they are not interested in. Persuasion gets people to do things that benefit the two parties involved.

Everyone can be persuaded, given the right context and timing. Political campaigns, for example, will focus their resources on a small group of people who are expected to swing voters during elections. The first part of persuasion is getting the right people to show your point of view first.

Context creates a standard for what is acceptable, while timing dictates what people want from life and others. For example, you might choose to marry a different person from who you date because the things you want change.

Finally, to be persuaded, you have to be interested. It is impossible to convince someone who has no interest in what you have to say. The first art of persuasion is knowing how to talk to people consistently and how to keep their attention.

General rules

Reciprocity is compelling. Providing a small gesture of consideration to other people sets the stage that if you ever ask for something in return, they are willing to offer it.

A person who is intent on asking for what they need while demonstrating value is more persuasive for their persistence. History is filled with people who managed to sway the masses in their favor because they were persistent. Abraham Lincoln first lost his mother, a sister, his girlfriend, and three sons. He failed in business and lost eight elections before he became president of the United States.

If you choose to compliment, be sure that your compliments are sincere. Compliments will affect your experience with a person. You are more likely to trust someone if you have good feelings while with them. If you want to persuade, do not compliment insincerely to get what you want.

Set and manage expectations. A considerable part of persuasion is managing what other people expect of you. It is ensuring that people can trust your judgment. A CEO who promises a 20% increase and delivers 10% more is rewarded while one who promises a 40% increase and provides 35% will be punished. Persuasion is about understanding other people's expectations and over-delivering.

To offer value to someone, do not assume that you know what they need. In sales, for example, it is more effective to sell to someone something they need. If you are unsure, ask people to tell you. Alternatively, offer people what you have and leave them to choose to take it or leave it.

Create urgency and scarcity. Different from the things people need to survive, everything else will have a relative scale of value. You will want things because other people do. Making an object scarce, even if that object is yourself, increases its value. Instilling a sense of urgency to the scarce item makes it that people take action immediately. If you are not motivated to want something quickly, it is unlikely that you would want it in the future.

Build rapport with people. Rapport extends beyond the conscious decisions to unconscious behaviors. In matching and mirroring the habitual behaviors of other people, you build a sense of rapport, and people feel more open to the suggestions you give. Telling the truth also helps to build rapport. Here, you would say to them the things about themselves that other people are unwilling to say. Truth-tell without any agenda or judgment, and you will find the results to be surprising.

Personal skills

In any interaction, it is the person who is most flexible who is in control. Children will often be persuasive because they can go through many behaviors to get what they need while parents only have 'no' to offer in response. If you have an extensive repertoire of actions, you are more persuasive.

Some people drain our energy while others infuse it. People considered the most persuasive know how to transfer energy to others. They know how to invigorate and motivate. Sometimes one can do this through eye-contact, laughter, and physical touch while other times, active listening works well.

It is not enough to listen, though; you have to be willing to explain your point of view and your concept in simple terms. The art of persuasion is about simplifying something to its core and then communicating it to other people.

Being prepared will give you an advantage. In this case, preparation is knowing about the situations around you and the people you interact with. Prepare meticulously if you want to be persuasive. For example, in a job interview, you have better chances of getting the job if you know about the background, services, and products the company you want to work in has.

If you find yourself in conflict, stay calm, and detach. When emotion is heightened, the person who can detach has the most leverage. People will turn to the people who can control their emotions to lead them. If you have to use anger, for instance, use it purposefully. Escalating a situation could help you by causing others to back down and providing an opportunity to present your argument.

Whatever the circumstance, be confident. A person with an unbridled sense of certainty will find it easy to persuade others. Believing in what you do will give you this sense of confidence.

Subtle ways to be persuasive

Gentleness in persuasion is an art. It is how people get the thing they want without appearing self-centered, needy, or demanding. The following are subtle ways you can be persuasive:

Know what you want
You cannot get what you want if you do not know precisely what you desire. The more defined you have your end-goal to be, the easier time you will have arguing for your case. Most people begin missing the mark when they only have a rough idea of what they could want but will not take the time to figure it out. Narrow down your expectations and

identify the options that fit what you want. Consider also how flexible you are willing to be before walking into any negotiation. Deal with challenges with a clear mind.

Be kind
There is a famous saying about catching more flies if you use honey and vinegar. This is true when it comes to persuasion. People are more likely to find solutions if others treat them with respect, value their time, and are pleasant to them. Be careful that you do not come off as insincere.

Act the part
Other times, all you need to do is behave as if you already have the thing that you want. If you want a promotion, for example, it may be helpful for you to dress and talk as if you have your desired role. There is a common phrase tossed around 'dress for the job you want.'

Acting the part is also about projecting confidence and showing that you believe in what you are doing enough to push others out of your way. Use body language cues like eye contact. Insecure and shy people will typically shrink when they meet people they esteem to be more believable and competent.

Confidence is also connected with being proactive. If you wait for other people to give you what you want, they may take a long time. When you want something, make changes in your life that make it possible for you to get that thing you want. These changes can be social, emotional, physical, or mental.

Finally, confidence will also be reflected in how direct you are. Getting right to the point will help you know the answer up front. However, if you choose to go this way, be sure you have the right person. Be sure also that you know the reasons you deserve what you are asking for.

What then do you do when persuasion fails?

Even the most persuasive people do not always get what they want. Part of knowing how to handle life is knowing how to respond when you do not get the thing you wish for. The next chapter tackles emotional intelligence and is designed to answer this question.

Chapter 4: An introduction to emotional intelligence

Two thousand years ago, Plato wrote that 'all learning has an emotional base.'

Since then, scientists, philosophers, and educators have worked to disprove or prove the place of feelings in learning and life. Unfortunately, for a big part of the past two millennia, the overarching idea was that 'emotions stand in the way of making good decisions and they keep people from focusing.' The last decade has seen the rise of research to dispute that idea.

This chapter explores how emotions have been viewed throughout history, what academia says about it with the hope of persuading you on the importance of emotional intelligence. Toward the end, the chapter steps out of academia into the realm of practical wisdom and helps you to apply the theory to life.

The definition of emotional intelligence

In the early 1950s, Abraham Maslow wrote about people enhancing their mental, spiritual, physical, and emotional strengths. His work began a conversation on 'human potential' that became celebrated mainly as part of humanism. In the 1970s and 1980s, new sciences developed that looked to study human capacity.

Scientists began conducting serious research to define intelligence and emotions. Since then, research has informed the changing beliefs on emotions and intelligence. Where once intelligence was about perfection, it became about recognizing that there was more to life. Where emotion was about suffering and eternal damnation, people started realizing that there might be more value to it.

Consequently, a conversation started that pitched head and heart against each other. The question would be framed as head over heart or heart overhead. In the 1990s, a consensus was reached, and an article was published that defined emotional intelligence as scientifically testable. The team that published the article would go on to publish more content on the subject.

Emotional intelligence is the ability to see emotions, to access and generate them to help thought, to understand emotional knowledge and feelings, and to regulate such emotions to support intellectual and emotional growth.

Emotional intelligence is made of four parts:

- *Perceiving emotion*

Emotional perception is about having the abilities and capacities to recognize and identify the feelings of other people in addition to the physiological and biological processes involved. Emotions have three components; cognitive appraisal, physical changes, and subjective experiences. Perceiving emotion is being able to make accurate decisions about another person's subjective experience by interpreting their physical changes through your sensory systems. Your neural systems have to be alert enough to translate the observed changes into mental representations.

In that sense, the ability to perceive emotion is innate but also subject to environmental influence. It is critical to social interactions. How feeling is interpreted and experienced will depend on the way it is perceived. Similarly, how emotion is seen will depend on a person's past experiences and interpretations.

Nonetheless, emotion is perceived audibly, visually, through bodily sensations and smell. The process of collecting this emotion is different from that used in perceiving non-emotional material.

Emotional perception is about noticing body language and other nonverbal cues. For example, a mother can see their child sucking his fingers and conclude hunger or fear, depending on the context.

- *Emotional reasoning*

Emotional reasoning is about using emotion to help thought. In this process, a person concludes that their emotional reaction communicates something true regardless of the evidence to the contrary. For instance, a spouse could have shown nothing, but devotion but a person using emotional reasoning concludes that 'I know that my spouse is unfaithful because I feel jealous.'

Emotional reasoning will amplify the effects of someone's cognitive distortions. For example, a person feeling insecure about their ability to understand a subject, even if they have the capability, may interfere with their performance because of the insecurity. If they act on their insecurity, they might assume that they misunderstand the material. So they may as well answer the questions randomly, and therefore, their fear becomes a self-fulfilling prophecy.

In emotional intelligence, the idea is to develop this process so that one does not lean into their cognitive biases. It involves using emotions as they present to guide prioritizing and thinking. For example, an emotionally intelligent parent may use his feelings to prioritize activities with his family.

- *Emotional awareness*

Emotional awareness or understanding emotions is about observing what one is feeling. Are you curious? Are you hopeful? Do you find something boring? Is it a distraction?

Emotions are part of the human experience. They provide useful information about what you are experiencing and help people know how to react. From birth, people sense their emotions. Children learn how to respond to those emotions using facial expressions or actions like crying, laughing, or cuddling. They can feel those emotions even before they can name them.

As you grow up, you begin to understand emotions, and instead of reacting like little kids, you can identify those emotions and verbalize them. With time and with enough practice, you get better at knowing the things you feel and why you feel them. This is emotional awareness.

Emotional awareness helps you to know what you want and what you do not want. It helps to build better relationships. When you are aware of your emotions, you can talk about feelings clearly and openly to avoid conflict and resolve it better when it arises.

Some people are more in touch with their emotions than others. The process of socialization causes some to repress some emotions or tag shame to others, making it hard for them to communicate openly.

If you have ever been in a situation where you wished you understood what someone was thinking, you wanted to understand emotions. Emotional awareness helps to articulate one's thoughts and helps you to look beyond someone's irrational behavior to see the underlying cause. An emotionally intelligent parent may, for example, realize that a child is throwing a tantrum, not to misbehave, but expressing frustration at being denied a treat.

- *Managing emotions*

Emotion management is the ability to accept one's feelings readily and to control them successfully in themselves and others. It is the ability to master your own emotions. Here, it is not enough to be open about your feelings and thoughts. You must also take control over changing those feelings and thoughts. It is recognizing that emotions are generated whenever an event or a person touches your values. Changing one's feelings and thoughts helps to prevent reactive outbursts.

Imagine being in a situation where you work hard for weeks, and your project is canceled. Alternatively, imagine having many assignments and being swamped with work or even having a customer unduly shout at you at work. Stressful situations as this will happen at the workplace and how you respond speaks to your ability to manage emotions.

Do you shout back at customers? Do you hide in a corner and begin feeling sorry for yourself? Do you distract yourself by playing games or chatting with people around the office?

The idea behind managing emotions is being able to mitigate behavior while keeping your productivity and efficiency. In developing emotional intelligence, a parent would, for example, be prepared to regulate their emotions when their child tries them to respond appropriately and model appropriate responses to their child.

Emotional intelligence is neither the opposite of intelligence nor the triumph of heart overhead. It is finding the sweet spot between the two and using it in everyday interactions.

Medieval theories of emotions

The Greek word pathos was used in ancient philosophies to refer to all feelings. The corresponding Latin names used for the same were affectio, passio, or affectus. Medieval theories of emotions were based on ancient sources. New development discussed feelings from the perspective of Avicennian faculty psychology. It was an extrapolation of Aristotelianism and was supported by detailed studies of the involuntary and voluntary aspects of emotional reactions.

Plato introduced the philosophical analyses of emotions. In his book, Republic, he divided the soul into three; the spirited part, the appetitive part, and the rational part. The terminology was to be later used by Aristotle and other philosophers even though their background assumptions varied.

The Latin terms for the parts were concupiscibilis, intellectus, and irascibilis. Plato viewed emotions as negative, except for love. He considered emotions to be irrational reactions to lower levels of the soul, of which the appetitive part sought pleasure while avoiding suffering. He argued that the spirited part housed aggression and self-affirmation.

According to him, the immaterial reasoning part was responsible for the rational will and knowledge. It was designed to govern and control spontaneous suggestions of the spirited part to support ethical conduct.

Plato assigned the emotional parts a non-intellectual cognitive evaluation with respect to representations and perception. He considered them as accompanied by an unpleasant feeling related to impulses that initiate action. His main reason for this idea was acrasy. He argued that if undisturbed, the knowledge of ethical conduct causes people to behave appropriately. The lower impulses, when uncontrolled, cause people to behave in other directions different from the good. They typically move toward aggression or immediate pleasure.

The different aspects that Plato tied to the movements of the lower soul were taken up by Aristotle and discussed in his theory of emotions as an integral part of the human condition.

Aristotle came up with a model for analyzing the psychological structure of emotions. It included four aspects. The first cognitive element he identified is unpremeditated evaluation or phantasy. Here, he supposed that something could happen to someone in a way that concerned them. The effective element was discussed as a pleasant or unpleasant feeling that someone experiences about evaluating content. The dynamic element was described as an impulse towards an action that accompanies emotional evaluation. The final element was the physiological reactions you experience, such as the changes in heartbeat or shaking of the legs at the knees.

The Aristotelian approach became influential to Western thought. The first element was cited in most medieval and ancient theories that talked about cognitive functions. They associated evaluative representation with an emotion.

Stoics, through their reason-centered approach, argued that emotions were to be treated as mistaken value judgments. This view became common and differentiated between non-emotional intellectuals and lower emotional parts of the soul. The prevailing view lasted for a while before it was overtaken by the Franciscan view of passions of the will.

Aristotle suggested that education could change someone's emotional dispositions so that their inclinations and evaluations support the quest for living well, instead of disrupting it. This idea formed a basis for Aristotle's theory of virtues, which included the sensory soul and good emotional habits as a function of practical reason. Part of his philosophical psychology considered the rational part of the soul as co-operating with the sensory part.

Aristotle and Plato presented a list of emotions, but they did not develop naming for those emotions except considering some as resulting from the appetitive part of the soul. The feeling aspect was always associated with emotional representation, and so Aristotle distinguished pleasant and unpleasant feelings.

The Stoics divided emotions into four types, varying based on whether the subject was seen as future good, present good, future evil, or present evil. They produced a long list of emotions that have since been quoted in many works like Boethius' Consolation of Philosophy. Their view of emotions, however, did not attract followers.

A well-known part of their philosophy included the works of Epictetus, Cicero, and Seneca as the therapy of emotions. Therapy aimed at removing emotions as a result of learning to see things according to the stoic view of objective reality that has no self-centered commitments. Emotions were seen as false judgments and reactions to these judgments. The stoics talked about the types of emotions as psychosomatic reactions. They regarded positive beliefs about the corresponding actions as irrational.

Other philosophers like Plutarch followed Plato's philosophy and argued for moderating emotions. The apatheia was seen as impossible and inhumane because it involved the disappearance of the emotional part. Earthly emotions were seen as useless in some spheres.

Later on, other theologians combined Platonist and Stoic ideas. They argued for freedom from emotion as part of Christian perfection and as a precondition for being made like the divine. The mystical union was criticized as a highly emotional language. Supernaturally caused feelings during spiritual experiences were exempt from the definition — one theory combined divine love with freedom from the mundane. A later version of this approach stressed moderation in everyday life.

Monastic literature on mysticism analyzed subjective feelings. Bernard of Clairvaux called it a sense of being affected by the divine. Other theologians like Thomas Aquinas taught on mystical experience as part of Christianity.

Monastic psychology also relied on Stoic doctrine and the Christian conception of sin. The Stoic idea stated that even apathetic people could react emotionally on exceptional occasions, but this would not be considered emotion because it did not involve judgment. Augustine taught that sin, in the thought process, was tied to the original sin and kept showing up in someone's mind.

According to him, the original fall came accompanied by shame that Adam and Eve felt when they were moved by the lower soul. He argued that they should not have let its function control them. He explained the original disobedience of the higher parts of the soul as the inherited sinful mode and the lower part as a relative autonomy that reminds people of their shameful condition.

Augustine taught that spontaneous responses in emotion were agitations and did not involve assent to behavioral suggestions. According to him, Stoics did not have a full picture of emotions because they were proud. He thought that evil desires and thoughts occur involuntarily. Temptations are, therefore, not accountable sins, and one should confess immediately; otherwise, they have consented to sin. His doctrine later developed into a detailed theory of the degrees of mortal and venial sin. Before his approach, sinful orientations were regarded as venial sins.

Love and compassion were also central in medieval theology. In the Vulgate translation of the Bible, there was a term for divine mercy and human sorrow. Compassio came to be coined later and used by Christian authors. Words were continually introduced as literature evolved to accommodate new world views.

It was always assumed that God did not have emotional pity or sorrow. Augustine thought of pity as a kind of compassion that compels people to help others. Later thinkers were to agree with the definition but tie compassion to charity. Aquinas later quoted Augustine saying that compassion was ethically neutral, and added that a person should be helpful in effect and compassionate in affect.

The history of emotional intelligence

When looking at emotional intelligence, it is critical to acknowledge the influence of ancient philosophies on modern philosophies. While the term emotional intelligence is new relative to the history of psychology and philosophy, a lot of the principles borrow from classical works.

Currently, many businesses appear to be drifting toward implementing some form of emotional intelligence coaching, training, and strategies with the hope of improving the perceptions and behavior of policymakers. The move also helps to eliminate preconceptions, biases, partialities, prejudices, and predispositions.

Unfortunately, a failure to know enough about emotional intelligence could stand in the way of noble efforts. Day to day operational procedures need to adjust, but so do marginal processes like policy-making and recruitment processes. If not implemented in that way, then emotional intelligence will not improve the workplace.

Part of this process is considering the recent history of emotions and emotional intelligence.

All through history, behavioral scientists shared definitions, connotations, meanings, and descriptions of emotions. While many of the studies concentrated on emotions experienced in the workplace, such emotions indeed can also be seen in other social settings.

The contextual construction of emotional intelligence started in the 19th century.

In 1877, a philosopher, Henry Noble day, used emotional intelligence to examine practical and contemplative unification of intelligence and feeling. He argued that intelligence and sentiment are related regardless of the type – whether patriotic or religious sentiments. He concluded that a person's mental processes are dominated by interconnectedness between endeavor, feelings, and intelligence.

In 1880, another philosopher explored how the mind is connected by volition or behavior, emotions, and intellect. He found that emotions and feelings were cognitively interconnected with the relationship between morality, self-emotions, and beliefs.

In 1910, a psychologist, James Sully, relied on the context of emotional intelligence to describe how the mental process is connected to the emotional process. He combined intellectual and emotional experiences and modified how scientists thought about the link between the two.

Ten years later, another scientist studied the variances between intellect from interactions and situations. He found there to exist three types of intelligence; abstract intelligence, mechanical intelligence, and social intelligence.

Another psychologist connected guidance and intelligence. He found an organic relationship between intelligence and emotions. Harriet Babcock studies how significant emotions were to abilities, self-confidence, and influence and found them to be integral to leadership. He examined the predominating surroundings that influence emotion and how they affect behavior and a person's ability to deliver.

In 1961, another study listed the predictors of interpersonal skills and abilities as variances that can be attributed to social intelligence. Emotions were found to be essential for constructing differential accuracy. They were found to be integral to social and academic intelligence. A different study found feelings to be necessary for problem-solving, social effectiveness, and performance.

In 1973, two scholars considered the development and measurement of social intelligence. They compiled many concepts and meanings focused on social intelligence and the ability to form perceptions, judgments, and behavior. They found that the central core of emotional intelligence was the ability to understand thoughts, emotions, and the intentions of other people.

In 1983, another scholar proposed theories of intelligence and defined a level of performance that was dependent on execution. The study included cognitive developmental psychology and the creation of a study model for intellectual competencies in many cultural settings. He sought to help policymakers to understand human intelligence.

In 1990, another study considered emotional intelligence as a tool for improving the quality of life. The scientists describe emotional intelligence as something that could be learned and enhanced towards improving one's quality of life.

In the same year, Daniel Goleman introduced the dimensions of emotional intelligence and argued for their importance in strong interrelationships.

Components of emotional intelligence

According to research from the past three decades, emotional intelligence is the combination of emotion and intelligence. It has the following elements as introduced by Daniel Goleman:

- *Self-awareness*

Self-awareness is the capacity to recognize and understand feelings. It is the ability to sense how one's actions, moods, and emotions will affect other people.

A self-aware person will be able to track their emotions to notice different emotional reactions and to identify their feelings accurately.

Self-awareness is also about realizing the connection between what one does and how they feel. A self-aware person has a sense of their limitations and strengths.

Self-awareness is also associated with openness to new ideas, experiences, and learning from social interactions.

Self-regulation

This aspect of emotional intelligence is about appropriately expressing emotion.

It includes being flexible, the ability to cope with change, and being able to manage conflict. It also covers the ability to diffuse difficult situations while still aware of how one's actions affect other people. Self-regulation also includes taking ownership of one's actions.

Social skills

An emotionally intelligent person will be able to interact with other people well. They can apply their understanding of emotions to themselves and to other people to interact and communicate with them in everyday situations.

Social skills range from verbal communication, active listening, and leadership, developing rapport, and non-verbal communication skills.

Empathy

Empathy is the ability to understand other people's feelings.

It is the component of emotional intelligence that allows someone to respond to other people appropriately after recognizing their emotions.

A person with empathy can sense the power dynamics that are at play in a social relationship. They recognize how these dynamics make people feel and can use these perceptions to influence behavior.

Motivation

Motivation as a component of emotional intelligence is intrinsic. It means that a person is driven to meet their goals and needs intrinsically rather than being motivated by external rewards like recognition, money, and fame.

Intrinsically motivated people experience a state of 'flow' when they are immersed in an activity. They are more action-oriented than their counterparts, and they need achievement. They are always looking to improve themselves and will likely be more committed to taking the initiative.

Models and frameworks of emotional intelligence

Gardner proposed the earliest theory of emotional intelligence. His conception of personal intelligence includes feelings. It does not focus on a sense of appraisal for others and a sense of self. It is focused on recognizing the use of emotional states in problem solving and behavior regulation.

There are three primary models of emotional intelligence, including:

Goleman's performance model

According to Goleman, emotional intelligence is about a group of competencies and skills focused on relationship management, self-awareness, and social awareness. He suggests twelve subscales, including self-awareness, self-control, adaptability, positive outlook, influence, empathy, achievement orientation, conflict management, inspirational leadership, organizational awareness, influence, and teamwork.

Bar-On's competencies model

Bar-On suggested that emotional intelligence is a system of behavior arising from social and emotional competencies. He argues that skills influence behavior and performance. His model consists of self-expression, self-perception, stress management, and decision making. It has 15 subscales, including self-actualization, self-regard, emotional self-awareness, problem-solving, reality testing, impulse control, and flexibility, among others. Bar-On suggested that these competencies drive human behavior and relationships.

Mayer, Salovey and Caruso's model

This model suggests that the information one perceives is from understanding and managing emotions. This information facilitates decision making. The four-branch model includes sensing emotions, using them to drive thought, understanding emotions, and managing those emotions. It is the model used for the remaining part of this book.

Signs of high emotional intelligence

Reading academia about emotional intelligence can make the subject seem detached and far from practical. Every sort of intelligence signals the ability to negotiate a specific set of challenges well. Someone who is smart but has messed their personal lives, or someone wealthy but challenging to work with, lack the same thing – emotional intelligence.

In this sense, they lack the quality that enables them to negotiate with insight, temperance, and patience, central problems in interpersonal relationships, and when relating to the self. In partnerships, emotional intelligence may show up as sensitivity to other people's needs, readiness to understand what could be going on beyond the surface, and to adopt for a moment someone else's point of view.

Concerning ourselves, emotional intelligence is about how one deals with envy, anxiety, professional confusion, and anger. It is what will distinguish people who are crushed by failure and those who can greet trouble with a melancholic and almost darkly humorous resilience.

You may have a high emotional intelligence if you exhibit the following characteristics:

- *Thinking about feelings*

Emotional intelligence starts with social awareness and self-awareness. It innately can recognize emotions and how they affect yourself and other people.

Awareness has to start with reflection. Ask yourself questions such as:

a) What are my emotional weaknesses? What are my strengths?
b) How does my mood now affect my decision making and my thoughts?
c) What are other people thinking, and what influences their words and actions?

Thinking about questions such as this can produce valuable insights that you can use to your advantage.

- *Pausing in difficult situations*

Pausing is about taking a moment to think before acting or speaking. It is difficult in practice, especially in emotionally charged situations, but it can save you from embarrassments or committing too fast.

Pausing helps to refrain from making permanent choices based on temporary emotions.

- *Striving to control your thoughts*

You have little control over the feelings you experience at any one moment. However, you can control how you react to your emotions by concentrating on your thoughts.

Emotionally intelligent people will work to control what they think. They resist enslavement to their emotions, allowing themselves to live in harmony with their values and goals.

- *You learn from criticism*

No one enjoys receiving negative feedback. However, you may be emotionally intelligent if you recognize criticism as a chance to learn even if it is delivered ungraciously. Even when that criticism is unfounded, it allows you to see into the thoughts of other people.

Learning from criticism is about being able to receive feedback, control your emotions, and consider how the feedback can make you better.

- *Showing authenticity*

Authenticity is not about sharing every personal detail to all people at all times. It is about saying what you mean and meaning what you say. It is about sticking to your principles and values more than anything else.

Authenticity is about knowing that the people who matter will appreciate your feelings and thoughts.

- *You show empathy*

Showing empathy is about understanding the inner feelings and views other people have and how they help you to connect with them. Empathy is resisting judgment or labeling other people's thoughts. It is working to see things from their perspective.

Empathy does not mean agreeing with the perspective of the other person, but understanding where they come from.

- *You praise others*

Every person craves appreciation and acknowledgment. When you compliment other people, you meet that craving and help build trust with them.

All this begins with focusing on the good in other people and then sharing the specific things that you like about them to inspire them to be their best.

- *You give helpful feedback*

Negative feedback can hurt the feelings of other people. Knowing this and being careful to reframe criticism can make the emotionally intelligent person. The idea is to help the recipient to see what you say as helpful and not harmful.

- *You apologize*

Apologizing from a place of understanding and acknowledging one's mistakes takes courage and strength. In doing so, you show humility, which is a quality that draws other people to you.

Emotional intelligence helps you know that apologizing is placing a value on the relationship more than the ego.

- *When you forgive, you forget*

Holding on to resentment is like leaving the knife inside after a stab. The offending party continues with their life, but you fail to allow yourself to heal.

When you forgive and forget, you make it possible that other people cannot hold your emotions hostage.

- *You keep commitments*

It is common practice for people to break their commitments or agreements whenever they feel like it. Of course, there is a difference between the impacts of breaking different types of commitments. When you make a habit of keeping your word, though, you develop a reputation of trustworthiness and reliability.

- *You help other people*

One of the ways to impact the emotions of other people positively is by helping them.

Most people are not concerned about your academic qualifications or your previous accomplishments. They care about the time you are willing to invest in listening to them and helping them out. They care about how prepared you are to work alongside them when it counts.

Such actions will create trust and inspire other people to follow suit when it matters.

- *You protect yourself against emotional sabotage*

Emotional intelligence has a dark side rooted in dark psychology. You may be emotionally intelligent if you recognize, for example, when other people try to manipulate you for a selfish cause or a personal agenda.

Improving your emotional intelligence

After reading through the signs, most people recognize a desire to improve their emotional intelligence. The following are ways to go about it:

- *Communicate assertively*

Assertive communication helps you to earn respect without appearing too passive or too aggressive. Emotionally intelligent people can communicate their needs and opinions directly without stepping on other people.

- *Respond to conflict instead of reacting*

During times of conflict, it is common to have emotional outbursts and to feel anger. An emotionally intelligent person can keep calm in stressful situations. They restrain from making impulsive choices that could escalate the problem. They know that during the conflict, the goal is resolution and so they choose to keep focused on aligning their actions and words to that.

- *Listen actively*

During conversations, the emotionally intelligent person will listen to gain clarity. They will not just be waiting for when it is their turn to speak. They ensure that they understand what the other person is saying before they can give a response. Pay attention to the non-verbal cues in the conversation. That way, you prevent misunderstandings and let the listener respond well. It communicates respect to the person you are addressing.

- *Stay motivated*

Emotionally intelligent people have an internal compass that keeps them motivated and rubs off on others. They set goals and stay resilient even when they face challenges.

- *Keep a positive attitude*

Your attitude can infect the other person. Emotionally intelligent people do not lose sight of this fact. They guard their attitude accordingly when with other people. They know what they need to do to have an optimistic outlook. This could include anything from meditating or engaging in prayer to keeping a collection of positive quotes in their workspace.

- *Be self-aware*

Emotionally intelligent people are intuitive. They know how their emotions are and how they affect the people they interact with. They also pick up on other people's body language to use that information to make communication better.

- *Receive critique well*

You are on your way to becoming emotionally intelligent if you can accept critique. Rather than getting defensive or offended, people with high EQ take time to understand where someone is coming from and evaluate the impact of their actions on performance. They are keen to know how to resolve issues constructively.

- *Demonstrate leadership*

Emotionally intelligent people show excellent skills for leadership. They have high personal standards and set examples for other people. They show initiative and are great at solving problems and making decisions, allowing them to be more productive.

- *Be friendly and approachable*

Emotionally intelligent people seem approachable to other people. They give off a positive presence. They know how to use their social skills based on the relationship they have with the person they interact with. Their interpersonal skills help them to communicate well.

Shifting worldviews and core beliefs

A worldview is the set of glasses you use to see the world. It is a mental model of reality – a comprehensive set of attitudes and ideas about the world, life, and yourself. It is a system of beliefs and personally customized theories about what the world is and how it works.

A worldview answers questions like what is the purpose of life? What are your goals? What are your values and priorities?

It also answers other existential questions like if God exists, the characteristics he has, and so forth.

Everyone has a worldview they have adopted. In most cases, people adopt their beliefs in reaction to an event that happens to them. Sometimes the process is conscious while other times it is not.

Even so, world views affect the decisions and actions you take in your everyday life. Your worldview will also be affected by attitudes, life situations, habits, and inherited characteristics.

Core beliefs, on the other hand, are fundamental beliefs that someone has about themselves. They are things that they hold as absolute truths underneath the surface. They are the filter through which you perceive and interpret the world.

Core beliefs sit at the back of the mind, and when an event happens, your brain opens up, consults that core belief, and helps you to defend yourself or acknowledge safety.

Core beliefs are convincing. They come filled with conviction and persuasion because you have accepted a core belief as absolute. This means that this belief will seem as true today as it was yesterday. These beliefs are so deep-seated that the mind structures your life around them without being conscious of them, questioning them, or even acknowledging them.

Core beliefs are essential in helping a person determine their degree of self-worth, competence, power, and love. In the same manner, negative core beliefs stand in the way of self-esteem and self-acceptance. The impacts will trickle to influence your sense of belonging and your view of how others treat you.

When it comes to emotional intelligence, core beliefs, and worldviews matter because they influence your internal state.

If a person who does not believe themselves to be worthy of affection compliments you, it will ring as insincere because you sense in them, a desire to manipulate, to get something else in return.

Earlier sections of this book have handled the actions that will help you judge if you are emotionally intelligent or not. They have explored ways you can improve your emotional intelligence. However, those ways must be built on a sure foundation; otherwise, they are just actions that will make people around you feel manipulated.

The next section of this book will look at the different beliefs that people have about emotions and emotional intelligence and will address ways to change them. The goal here is simple; if you change from the inside, you will not need to be so conscious of the actions you take on the outside.

Letting your authentic self-shine through will automatically communicate high emotional intelligence. The emotionally intelligent person primarily has a good relationship with themselves.

Think of emotional intelligence in this case as having a cup. The only way to serve people from that cup without losing yourself is to fill the cup so much that it overflows. In this analogy, losing yourself is akin to becoming manipulative and losing the feeling of being centered.

The following are common ideas you may need to explore within yourself to change them. Note that self-awareness and self-actualization are about choosing the worldviews and the core beliefs that you want to embody rather than letting life take its toll and responding however you may.

Negative emotions versus positive emotions

Most people make the mistake of assuming that positive psychology is about positive emotions. Of course, the study has a bent towards that, but the field is not just about positive emotions. Negative emotions are inevitable. Everyone needs to experience those so that their lives can be rich and full.

People who have been studying emotions for years place a heavy focus on feelings. The surprising part is often the lack of harmony between definitions, which leads to a failure to understand the necessity of all emotions for healthy functioning.

For the sake of this section, positive emotions will be considered as those that are pleasurable to experience. According to the handbook of positive psychology, desirable or pleasant situations yield pleasurable sensations and positive effects that have to be married to those situations to make sense.

According to this definition, positive emotions are a pleasant response to the environment or to our internal dialogue that are more sophisticated than pure sensations.

Conversely, negative emotions are feelings that are not pleasurable to experience. They are unpleasant or unhappy and are invoked when a person expresses a negative effect toward a person or an event.

An emotion that drags you down or discourages you is a negative emotion, by this definition.

Positive emotions vary depending on the person that you ask. Even how these emotions are defined will vary based on the person. However you define emotion, though, you have to accept that discerning between the two is intuitive. You 'just know' when your emotions are negative or positive.

Positive emotions are such as joy, love, contentment, interest, amusement, awe, satisfaction, and serenity. Negative emotions are such as anger, disgust, annoyance, loneliness, sadness, rage, and melancholy.

Consider the list of negative emotions. Is there any one of them you want to feel? How about the positive ones? Which ones do you wish you were experiencing? You will notice that even though you have experienced positive emotions at a time you thought you should not be experiencing them, they are typically pleasurable. They are necessary to thrive and grow.

If then it is universally accepted that negative emotions are unpleasant and undesirable, are they necessary?

Negative emotions are necessary because they provide a counterpoint to positive emotions. That is, if you have no negative emotions, positive emotions will not feel as good. Secondly, negative emotions are evolutionary. They encourage you to act in ways that boost survival chances and help growth.

This is to say that there is a good reason for experiencing every emotion. Anger helps in fighting against problems. Fear serves protection while anticipation helps to plan. Surprise helps one to focus on new situations, and joy reminds you of what is essential in life. Trust tells you who to connect with, and sadness connects you to the people you love. Disgust helps you reject the things that are unhealthy.

If you did not have fear, would you have known to protect yourself? Would you have identified the risks before committing to a particular activity? Without disgust, would you refrain from doing some things?

Negative emotions serve a purpose in life.

It is also common to imagine that stress is a solidly negative emotional response to different situations. However, people can experience stress in positive and neutral situations.

Many experiences that people think of as positive also contribute to stress. For example, brides get stressed when planning a wedding. People might get anxious about planning a move, the holidays, or having a baby. It could be nerve-wracking to start a new job.

It is, therefore, natural to feel stress in any situation even though you would classify the situation as positive or negative. The two play an integral role in balancing life.

Having established that the two emotions are vital for a healthy life, how do they affect you?

Negative and positive emotions all affect the brain.

Positive emotions increase the performance of a task by lifting our mood without being a distraction like negative emotions. They trigger reward pathways in the brain and therefore contribute to lower levels of the stress hormones and improve your well-being. They also help you to broaden your horizons and widen the scope of focus for the brain.

Meanwhile, negative emotions facilitate conflict processing. They help you to make sense of conflicting and incongruent emotional information, allowing you to figure out tough emotional problems. They also promote the understanding of confusing signals that you receive. Finally, negative emotions reduce empathy, which helps to protect you from being too involved with other people and staying focused on your goals.

The roles of positive and negative emotions in the brain are complementary and not competitive.

Considering how impactful both positive and negative emotions are on behaviors and thoughts, one can see why positive psychology monitors negative emotions. Since one needs to boost their positive emotions and take advantage of the benefits they bring, they also have to learn how to adapt negative emotions so that they can cope effectively.

When you can accept and embrace the two types of emotions, you give yourself a chance to live a meaningful and balanced life.

More importantly, though, for the individual and their emotional well-being, they have to be willing to take off the labels from the emotions they experience.

Emotional intelligence and shame

You experience shame when your behavior or emotional response falls short of your principles or the expectations other people have of you, and you label that response as wrong.

Shame is considered a negative emotion but is often the one responsible for the many people who are unable to live emotionally healthy lives.

One of the critical problems is that people cannot differentiate between shame and guilt. Guilt is adaptive, and it is helpful. It is holding something up against your values and feeling the psychological discomfort it causes.

Shame, on the other hand, is connecting guilt with identity. It is believing that you are flawed and therefore unworthy of belonging and love or believing that what you have done makes you unworthy of connection.

Guilt is productive and helpful, while shame is not. Unwatched, shame leads to destructive and hurtful behavior that causes further disconnection.

Understanding the differences between guilt and shame is essential in informing emotional intelligence. It will change the way one parents themselves and others. It will alter how you engage in relationships and how you give feedback.

Research has been done about language and labeling. Researchers do not need to look through the lens of guilt and shame to evaluate different constructs, but they agree that language is tied to a feeling of shame and discomfort around negative emotion.

In a series of experiments, participants were asked to claim money they had not earned at the expense of the researchers. They had to meet two conditions in each experiment, but the difference in the conditions was how the instructions were worded. In the first condition, they were told that researchers wanted to know 'how common cheating was on campuses,' and in the second, they were told that researchers wondered 'how common cheaters are on campuses.'

The difference is subtle, but it meant varying results. Participants under the first condition claimed they collected more cash than in the second. This was found true for both online interactions and face-to-face conversations showing that anonymity did not displace the implications of people self-identifying as cheaters. People could allow themselves sometimes to cheat, but they were not open to identifying as cheaters.

If you want to create a meaningful shift in the way you experience emotions and the way you respond to other people's, you have to understand the clear differences between guilt and shame. If you move away from shame, you will walk away from the practice of labeling yourself for a particular emotion and toward being emotionally healthier.

Psychological projection

People who are not self-aware enough to recognize shame when it shows up will easily project their emotions on to other people and cause situations that might have been easy to resolve to escalate.

Psychological projection is a subconscious defense mechanism that people use to cope with difficult emotions and feelings. It involves projecting undesirable emotions onto someone else instead of admitting and dealing with them.

Imagine disliking someone, and instead of admitting it, you start imagining that they have a vendetta against you. That is an example of projection.

The theory of projection was developed by Sigmund Freud, who is often referred to as the 'father of psychoanalysis.' During his sessions with patients, he noticed that sometimes they would accuse other people of the feelings they were demonstrating. By engaging in this behavior, the patient could better deal with the emotions they were experiencing.

An example of projection is a woman who was unfaithful to her husband, and so she accuses him of cheating. In another case, someone could feel compelled to steal and so project that feeling onto other people. She might start fearing that her purse would be stolen and that she would be shortchanged if she bought something.

Projection is not always dramatic. Sometimes, it is not even identifiable. An example of projection that many people relate to is when they meet someone they have no liking for, but they have to interact with them politely. Case in point; Jessica starts to resent her sister-in-law Carla for her close relationship with her husband. She knows that she has to act friendly to Carla for the sake of her husband. Over time, she starts to notice that Carla does not like her either.

Whenever they go to a family gathering, Jessica imagines Carla to be snippy with her when her husband is around. She explains to her husband that she has tried, but she does not understand why Carla does not like her. She has then projected her feelings of resentment and dislike onto Carla.

Projection is a defense mechanism, and as with all defense mechanisms, it helps to cope with emotions and feelings that you have trouble coming to terms with or expressing.

To extrapolate the example of Jessica and Carla, Jessica has difficulties accepting that she resents her sister-in-law. She may feel guilty for her feelings of jealousy, or she may feel shame at the thought that her feelings are noticed by the members of the family who will then think of her badly. Projecting her feelings onto Carla gives her an excuse for disliking her so that she does not have to face her feelings of resentment and dislike on her own.

Besides projection, other defense mechanisms you may commonly use include:

- Denial – refusing to admit to yourself that something is a reality, as in not believing your doctor when she tells you bad news about your health.
- Distortion – changing the reality of certain situations to meet the needs you have, such as thinking your boyfriend cheated on you because he was afraid of commitment.
- Passive aggression – acting out aggression indirectly, such as parking in your co-worker's parking spot as retribution for a dispute you had.
- Repression – covering up emotions or feelings instead of dealing with them, like when someone cannot remember the details of a car accident.
- Sublimination – converting negative feelings into positive ones such as cleaning your house whenever you feel angry.
- Dissociation –changing aspects of your personality substantially but temporarily to avoid feeling a particular emotion. An example is when you are trying to 'keep it together' at a funeral to benefit others.

Defense mechanisms are not always unhealthy. Sometimes, they are essential for coping with stressful events. Humor, for example, can be used as a positive defense mechanism for dealing with stress. Humor is a difficult situation that allows you to open up while pleasing others.

Most people do not realize when they are projecting until it is too late. However, there are steps you can take to make sure that you know when you are projecting and how to avoid doing it in the future.

It is good practice to start by looking at the negative relationships in your life. Which people do you not get along with, and why? Do you feel like someone is looking to harm you? Where did the animosity begin? In some cases, you could find that when you speak with a therapist openly, you can identify the emotions.

Once you find that you were projecting, you become more aware of this tendency as you interact with people in the future. Try to meet disputes and problems head-on instead of getting defensive. That way, you respond positively.

Note that projection is not always negative. Even though the Freudian theory assumes that you project undesirable feelings, one can also project positive feelings.

In complementary projection, for example, you assume that the other people share the same opinions that you have. This phenomenon is common. For instance, when you hear someone tell a story of a mistreated animal, you get shocked to find that not everyone thinks the same about animal cruelty as you. In the same way, even though you cannot see how people see color, you assume blue looks the same for everyone as it does you. In that sense, you are projecting your perception of color onto other people.

Complimentary projection is not very common. People who use it assume that others have similar abilities and skills as them. For instance, someone skilled in the kitchen assumes that everyone can make an omelet the way they do, and that is not always true.

Projection is not a healthy way to deal with emotions, but it is a difficult habit for people to break. It is much better to deal with the monsters in your head instead of projecting the feelings you experience.

Part of being able to deal healthily with emotions is admitting to yourself that it is natural to feel them as they present and to find a healthy outlet.

A different view of emotions

Abraham Maslow classified human needs into five kinds – safety needs, physiological needs, social needs, self-actualization needs, and esteem needs.

He developed a theory of motivation based on the hierarchy of needs.

The underlying assumption for his theory is that how someone behaves is driven by the urgency of their need. An individual would try to satisfy which ones of their needs are the strongest first. After it has been achieved, it would no longer motivate him, and so he would move to meet other needs.

Maslow described the different needs as follows:

- *Physiological needs*

These are needs, such as water, air, sleep, clothing, food, and shelter. They refer to needs that are essential to human survival. Without food, you would likely die of starvation. Physiological needs are biological, and they keep your body fit. There is a famous saying that anyone can live on bread even if they have no butter.

- *Safety needs*

After the physiological needs have been satisfied to a reasonable degree, one begins to worry about safety. For example, one may want to consider a pension for old age, job security, compensation for retrenchment, or getting an insurance plan. Security plays an essential role in choosing a job.

- *Social needs*

Social needs cover the need for affection, friendship, acceptance, and love by a group. A man is a social being and needs 'to be loved' and 'to love.' Workers form informal groups where they can have meaningful relationships with others. Management should be open to such groups as long as they do not affect the organization.

- *Esteem needs*

Esteem needs are concerned with a person's self-respect and self-confidence. They also touch on appreciation, approval, recognition, and status. The satisfaction of these needs will produce a feeling of confidence in people. People love to be praised for the work they do since it is recognition of their effort.

- *Self-actualization needs*

Self-actualization needs include self-development and self-advancement. They include the desire to take on more responsibilities. In a work environment, for example, an employee might want to develop and working under an unaware employer, they might start feeling restless. Maslow phrased this need as the desire to become more and more of what a person is – becoming everything you are capable of becoming.

Maslow's hierarchy of needs emphasizes three ingredients:

- A man is a social animal, and so has needs of many types.
- There is a hierarchy to those needs. That is, the needs will be arranged in preference so that after the lower level ones are met, the higher needs fall in place. A man with a full stomach will then notice other needs.
- A satisfied need will not motivate action. Only unsatisfied needs will influence human behavior.

In a different book, Dr. Gary Chapman talked about needs in terms of love languages.

The five languages describe the manners in which a person feels appreciated and loved. These love languages will vary with the personality type and the background of the person. The book suggests that one learns how to decode and understand the different ways of showing love to help them be able to care for the needs of their partner.

The love languages include:

- *Words of affirmation*

This love language understands love expressed as words to build your partner up. Verbal compliments do not need to be complicated to be effective. They can be something like 'your dress looks incredible on you' or 'you always make me laugh.'

For a partner whose primary love language is words of affirmation, words mean a lot. Compliments and an 'I love you' mean a lot. On the other hand, insulting comments and negative words can hurt them and take them longer to forget.

- *Acts of service*

For a partner whose primary love language is acts of service, 'actions speak louder than words.'

This love language shows itself by doing things that your spouse would like, such as doing laundry, cooking a meal, or picking up a prescription. All these things should be done as an expression of love and not actions out of obligation.

- *Receiving gifts*

This love language is not about materialism. It means that a thoughtful or meaningful gift would make your partner feel appreciated and loved. The gift could be as simple as bringing them ice cream after a long workday. Gifts differ from acts of service.

- *Quality time*

Quality time is about undivided attention. When you are giving your partner that time, there are no distractions – no smartphones, no televisions, etc. People whose primary language is quality time do not just want to be periodically involved with a thing or two. They want to be the center of your attention. They want you to look at them and only them.

Quality time does not mean that you don't relax to a movie; it means that you set apart time to be together without distractions to feel comforted in the relationship.

For such a person, every time you are not present in your time together or when you cancel a date, it translates as hurtful to them and makes them feel like you care more about other things than you do them.

- *Physical touch*

For people whose primary love language is physical touch, nothing is as impactful as touching them. They are not necessarily crazy about PDA, but they feel more connected and safer if the relationship involves hugging, holding hands, and kissing.

People with this primary language will feel unloved without physical contact. All the gifts and words in the world will not change anything. They want to feel close emotionally and physically.

One mistake a lot of people make when thinking about needs is looking outward. It is okay to look to meet the needs of another person, but you should also look inwards to ensure that you get your needs met.

An important fact to note about emotions is that they are the truest testament to where you are. If someone's comment makes you feel self-conscious, it has touched on something sensitive about you.

If you think of emotions that way, you will use them to help you identify which ones of your needs are not being met and look to meet those needs.

Note that negative emotions can also be an indication of a boundary that has been crossed. The boundary could be emotional, physical, or psychological and can be crossed outwards or inwards. Knowing the specific way, the boundary has been crossed helps you communicate well and set the boundaries where they should be.

In other cases, all you may need to do is use emotions to identify your core beliefs and see which beliefs you want to keep and which ones you want to do away with.

Identifying core beliefs

Core beliefs dictate how you live life. Everyone has them. They are formed in the early years of life and are based on the experiences and thoughts you have then. They are also influenced by the things you see others do and the advice you get when growing up.

Because core beliefs form in early life, they come steeped in adolescent and child-like thinking. There is nothing wrong with it, except one should know when the thought lacks the understanding and insight of adult life experiences.

Adolescent thinking can sometimes say to ignore the consequences, be self-centered, to favor immediate gratification, or to rely on prejudices and stereotypes. It may also lead you to rely on subjective and emotional rationales instead of being logical. It lacks flexibility and practicality.

Acknowledging one's core beliefs can help one to change them consciously and adapt to an adult lifestyle.

Core beliefs also affect how you interpret what happens to you and how you perceive the world. They color self-judgments and your judgments of other people. They form the rules that you live by, and so can affect self-worth, self-esteem, and self-acceptance.

A negative core belief could be something like:

'I am not good enough' and would be supported by a view that 'if people knew the truth about me, they would not like me.'

A surface thought that corresponds to this belief could say something like: 'I will not go to the party because I do not know anyone, and I would become shy and nervous.'

A positive core belief would affirm that you are good enough, encourage you to try and cheer you on. It is something like:

'I am competent and capable,' supported by a belief that 'I can do my job as well as any other person, and my colleagues know that.'

A surface thought could ask for a raise, knowing itself to be worth it.

Core beliefs are often distorted by trauma. This is because when a person is young, they respond to rejection, hurt, or trauma as seeing themselves as unworthy or flawed. This is also true for children who were neglected – if no one mirrored value to you, you may be unable to see it.

Whether you tell yourself that you are not good enough or that you are unworthy, you focus on the evidence to the contrary and discount the positives instead. Understandably, you continue to feel worse, and eventually, you become convinced that this is true. You become demotivated and no longer want to change anything.

On the other hand, reminding yourself of the times you have succeeded; when you worked hard, and it went well, you convince yourself that you are good enough. You begin to feel motivated and hopeful, and you give yourself opportunities to disprove of the negative core beliefs. You affirm, confirm and solidify the positive beliefs.

Core beliefs are the foundation of your self-worth. They dictate what you can do and what you cannot do, and they decide how you interact with the world. Changing them takes effort.

What then do core beliefs look like?

A core belief about you will show up as an 'I' statement as in 'I am unlovable.'

A belief could be that 'no one loves me' and is supported by a prediction belief about the actions others take (or have taken) when you do a certain thing.

You may argue for it even, saying that 'It's true, no one does!'

It could be that if it were not for the core belief, then you would be able to accept love, and you could be loved. It is also possible that other people responded as they did because of the negative core belief. It became a self-fulfilling prophecy.

A core belief about other people or the world takes the same format.

The following are examples of core beliefs:

- I am unlovable, so nobody will ever appreciate me
- I am smart, so if I try I will succeed
- The world is not safe, so I need to protect myself
- People are untrustworthy and will take advantage of me if I give them a chance

Part of learning to identify your emotions is finding your core beliefs. You can use the downward arrow technique that involves following the following questions to understand where the underlying assumption came from.

Begin by identifying a surface thought that you often have, such as, 'I procrastinate too much.'

Ask yourself, 'what does that say about me?'

The answer might read something like, 'I am afraid I will fail' or 'I am lazy.'

Ask yourself again what that says about you.

The answer could be 'I am a failure' or 'I am weak.'

If you ask yourself the question again, the core belief might be, 'I am not good enough.'

When trying to identify a core belief about other people, the question becomes, 'what does that say about women/family/men/people?' or 'what does that say about the world?'

After identifying the core issue and some unbalanced beliefs, start an inner self-dialogue that protects you from the pain of those beliefs.

You will have to start by learning to identify your thoughts, and once you find that there are some automatic thoughts you have in response to the beliefs, you can begin dealing with the situation as an adult. That way, you recognize the core issue and the core pain of your beliefs.

Many people will usually go about life taking their thoughts for granted. We are not taught to consider the thoughts we have and to know how they differ from our feelings.

Feelings can usually be described with one word that explains a collection of sensations or one sensation. For example, furious, thrilled, sad, or guilty are feelings.

Thoughts are more complex and will have many words. They are how you talk to yourself and what is typically going on through your head, such as 'my partner denies me affection.'

Some people experience their thoughts as commentaries in their heads. Others see them as words on paper while others see moving pictures or images like in memory. Memories are, themselves, a type of thought, and so is doing a mathematical equation of rehearsing a speech.

'Automatic thoughts' are intuitive and pop up as a response to something. For instance, if someone cuts you off as you drive, the thought that pops up might be that they are a jerk. When you recognize this thought, you can challenge it by responding that 'perhaps they didn't see me indicating.'

Since core beliefs are subjective, they cannot be proven or tested and so one has to do the job of identifying them on their own. However, the rules derived from the core beliefs can be tested. Most of the rules that core beliefs result in are self-protective and are designed to help us avoid catastrophe, trouble, and pain.

If you are afraid of failure, for example, your rules could be:

- Never expect to get ahead
- Never quit a job

- Never try hard at anything
- Never challenge the opinions of others

Breaking these rules could cause a catastrophe. For instance, what if you worked hard and you failed? It would prove challenging to confront the idea that 'I am a failure.'

If you believe yourself to be unworthy, your rules could be something like:

- Always strive to be perfect
- Never initiate contact with someone you like
- Always work extra hard
- Never say NO to anything
- Never admit to a mistake or fault

Adolescent thinking tricks you into thinking that by obeying these rules, you might avoid confronting the fact that you are unworthy.

In this sense, core beliefs are self-protective, but they may also deny you an opportunity to prove the belief incorrect.

Below is an exercise to help you identify your rules. Ensure that you start with identifying the core belief.

Step 1: Write your core belief on a paper.

Step 2: Read the checklist below and select the questions relevant to you. Ask them to yourself and answer honestly.

- How do you respond to other people's needs, requests, desires, anger, praise, criticism, disappointment, or withdrawal from you?
- How do you handle mistakes?
- How do you deal with problems, losses, or stress?
- What is your posture toward challenges and trying new things?
- How do you express your feelings, needs, anger, hopes and dreams, limits, and pain?
- How do you ask for help and support?
- How do you manage being with family, strangers, friends, and alone?
- Do you trust other people?
- Do you have friends?
- How do you respond to illness or health?
- Are you maintaining self-care?

As an example; someone whose core belief is that they are worthless could choose to answer the following:

- I deal with anger by trying to keep the peace, or withdrawing, and keeping quiet.
- I hint at my needs instead of asking directly. Otherwise, I become passive-aggressive.
- I don't disagree with people unless they are strangers
- I keep my anger to myself
- I deal with stress by avoiding making decisions or procrastinating action.

Step 3: Identify catastrophes that could happen if you broke the rules. For example:

- Speaking up could make the other person angrier. It would be my fault, and the relationship would end.
- If I express my needs, I might be rejected and realize that my needs are unimportant.
- If I disagree, I will be wrong, and everyone will know I am stupid.
- If I express anger, my feelings will be unacceptable.
- If I make decisions, I will do the wrong thing and make matters worse.

After this exercise, you have identified the rules your inner self has to protect you. After acknowledging your fears, you will need to change your core beliefs.

Changing core beliefs

How then do you do it?

Step 1:

Choose a core belief that you want to change and focus on the rules you have identified.

Consciously break down that rule and measure the outcomes. Consider it an experiment for your good.

You want to pick a rule that tests your core belief directly. You can start with a low-level fear to help you warm up. Ensure that the outcome of breaking that rule is measurable, and the behavioral result is clear, not just subjective feeling. Pick something whose outcome you can observe immediately.

Step 2:

Keep a prediction log. In there, write the catastrophic outcomes that could happen if you break a rule, write the experiment, and write the outcome.

Step 3:

Visualize and script your new behavior.

If your fear has to do with communication, practice an imagery test. You can act it out with someone or in a mirror. You could even video yourself doing the task and examine your posture and voice to get it right. Looking, sounding, blaming, or getting defensive would create an undesirable outcome.

Step 4:

Try out your new behavior and collect data about the outcome. Write your feelings and thoughts about the outcome.

Step 5:

Repeat the test and keep recording the results.

Step 6:

Rewrite your core belief as an affirmation. Keep it short and straightforward and write recommendations for replacing the old rules.

New rules could be something like:

- I can cope with conflict
- My needs are just as urgent as everyone else's
- I will stand up for the things I believe in
- I have good judgment and can solve problems
- I can solve problems by expressing anger in respectful ways

The primary reason to change your core beliefs toward developing emotional intelligence is to be secure in yourself as a person. If someone said your hair was grass and they started to laugh, would you feel hurt?

Perhaps not. You are only affected by what other people think if you suspect they might be right. Knowing their mental image of you is not you gives you immunity against their opinion.

Changing core beliefs and its impact on identity

One of the most common questions people ask when it comes to changing core values is the impact it will have on their identity and the comfort in which they exist.

If you have ever been to an interview, you know the feeling you get when asked to explain who you are.

Different from your name, you are likely to talk about the roles you play in your family, in society, in your past job, and the hobbies you have.

Other people even go deeper to talk about personality traits that they have that define their character.

The problem with the definitions is that as circumstances change, so does identity. When you lose your job, your values change, and you might begin to wonder whether your job was all that you were.

According to Eckhart Tolle, you are not anything. The self does not exist, but is instead, a projection of your mind, made of labels and stories. The philosopher congratulates people who can admit to not knowing who they are. According to him, you get a sense of peace when you stop trying to define who you are.

'Give up trying to define yourself. You will not die. You will come alive,' he says. In extending the argument, then defining yourself by thought is limiting.

People will often resist this idea by arguing for a need for direction or for something to stand for. 'If there is nothing I am working toward, what then am I doing?' they ask.

The key to accepting constant change is in admitting that life is not about who you are in the moment, but who you are living up to become.

As you choose what habits to strengthen and which ones to let go of, the question ceases to be 'who am I?' and becomes 'who am I becoming.' Nothing in this world remains unchanging except change. Even the cells in your body are constantly renewing themselves. Pinning yourself down to one thing makes life difficult because you are in a constant flux of change.

A better approach is to imagine yourself as a work in progress. That way, you do not define yourself as who you are but the person you are becoming. You envision a better self and then use it as inspiration. You then design and grow life to live in line with that vision.

The key to living this way is letting go of the idea of a static self and beginning to see yourself as becoming a new thing every day.

A growth mindset removes you from the trap of a fixed identity and imagining that there are things about you that you cannot change. There will always be a gap in life between who you want to be and who you are, and it often causes regret and frustration.

Regardless of genetic capabilities and past trauma, someone with a growth mindset can change and improve their abilities to become whoever they want to be.

Some theories explain changing your mindset as touching a switch to turn on the lights. This is true as far as it regards the effects of a changed mindset. However, the first stages of change are always difficult.

Developing emotional intelligence is about recognizing the need for change and committing to the process until you achieve one goal and are ready to meet the next challenge. Be careful not to buy into the idea that you can ever live in a state of self-actualization. The process of becoming is forever.

Myths and misconceptions about emotional intelligence

In the process of identifying core beliefs and changing, one may want to be sure they have the proper information about whatever it is they are shifting toward.

Even though emotional intelligence is a relatively new subject of study, there are still myths that have taken ground that may form resistance to change. Some of the most pervasive ones include:

- Emotional intelligence is a feminine or touchy-feely capacity – It is not true that emotional intelligence is innately true. It may be true that some women are more attuned to their emotions and so better able to develop the skills necessary to be emotionally intelligent, but that does not prove the point. Besides, going back in time to Greece, the ability to regulate or control emotions was considered masculine. Note that recent research shows both men and women to lack emotional intelligence in equal measure.

- Emotional intelligence is only useful for personal relationships – This myth has been perpetuated by personal development gurus and life coaches who think people's inability to control emotions to be a bad thing. They consider it destructive to the overall well-being of people. Emotional intelligence is as relevant in business and public life as it is in personal life.

- Emotional intelligence is only about caring for others and being empathetic – Emotional intelligence is first about self-awareness before it is about empathy. Empathy arises from such an in-depth knowledge of self that a person can recognize other people's emotions. A leader with emotional intelligence can, in an emotionally charged situation, control their emotions while diplomatically responding to the feelings of others.

- Emotional intelligence is a predictor of success in life – The craze over emotional intelligence is responsible for this myth. People have started to imagine it to be the only source of all problems in life. Emotional intelligence is helpful, but it is not the single ingredient you need to be successful. For example, people who have high IQ and an ability to comprehend technical problems, like professors and engineers, and have low emotional intelligence can become highly successful in life.

- Emotional intelligence is innate, you either have it, or you do not – the question of emotional intelligence is not a 'nature versus nurture' question. There are people with better emotional intelligence aptitude. However, the skill is learnable and can be honed with time. People can learn to recognize their emotional states and to see other people's nonverbal signals to help calm others down.

Chapter 5: Applying emotional intelligence to leadership

Leadership can be defined as the art of motivating a group to act toward a specific goal. In a business setting, it could mean directing colleagues and workers with a strategy that meets the needs of the company.

This definition captures the essentials, which include the ability to inspire others and the willingness to do so. Effective leadership is based on different ideas but will only happen if those ideas are communicated to the involved parties so that they can interact with them as the leader requires.

The leader must then be able to inspire and direct action. He must be the person in the group who combines both leadership skills and a personality that can help people follow his direction.

In business, leadership will also be connected with performance. While performance is not always about profit, the people that are seen as effective leaders are those who help a company toward its bottom line. If a person in a role of leadership fails to meet the expectations of profit by the shareholders or higher management, they may be terminated.

The terms 'management' and 'leadership' will then tend to find interchangeable use. Management, however, refers to the structure of leadership in a company or to people whose job description reads 'manager.'

On the other hand, leadership demands that one goes beyond management duties. To be effective, a leader has to manage the resources they have at their disposal, but they also have to supervise, inspire, and communicate.

There has been a common debate throughout decades whether leaders are born or made.

Some people appear to be naturally endowed with the ability to lead, but history has also shown that people can learn how to lead by improving specific skills.

History is filled with people who had no prior experience of leadership stepping up in crises and persuading others to follow their suggested course of action. They possessed qualities that allowed them to occupy those roles.

A simple search on the internet will prove the point. It will reveal, at least, the interest people have in learning how to lead with articles about leading so that people follow being at the top of search results. You will find that leadership falls along a bell curve. That fact alone supports the camp that believes leaders to be made.

One typical example is the former CEO of Apple, Steve Jobs. When he started the company in his garage in 1976 and his board of directors fired him nine years later, he disagreed with them on the direction the business would take in the future. After founding another company, Pixar, he was rehired as CEO and has developed the company as has come to be now known.

All accounts suggest that the mercurial genius routinely yelled at his co-workers, vendors, partners, and employees. Some former employees of his said he was intolerant and viewed failure with foul-mouthed tirades. He thought himself to be brutally honest and gave no regard to the feelings of his employees. He did not conduct reviews for his employees and hardly praised them for work well done.

According to biographies, the man has now matured, and his management style has become moderate. Some of his negative traits have worn off, and he displays empathy for other people. When he returned to Apple, he was forced to cut some of the staff members. He was quoted as expressing concern for the employees and their families. At the time of his death, the man was described in news articles as a visionary, innovator, genius and icon.

Theoretically speaking, leadership is the process of guiding, directing, and influencing the behavior of others toward meeting a particular goal. The leader has to be able to inspire zeal and confidence in other people. Leadership is characterized by:

- Interpersonal relations to influence others
- Qualities such as maturity and intelligence
- Involvement in a group
- Shaping behavior toward a vision
- A specific situation for context

Leadership helps to maximize efficiency and serves the following reasons:

- *Initiating action* – the leader starts by communicating the plans and policies to the subordinates where work starts.

- *Motivation* – they have to prove an incentivizing role. That way, the leader motivates employees with economic and non-economic rewards.

- *Providing guidance* – the leader has to supervise and guide their subordinates. Guidance, in this case, is about helping subordinates work efficiently and effectively.

- *Creating confidence* – Confidence is achieved by expressing efforts to subordinates and explaining their role while giving them guidelines to achieve their goals. They have to be willing to listen to the problems and the complaints of the employee.

- *Building morale* – morale refers to the willingness of employees to co-operate toward getting their work done. A leader has to win their trust to inspire them to use their abilities to achieve their set goal.

- *Building the work environment* – The leader has a responsibility to create an efficient environment for work and growth. Human relations should be part of the leader's job description.

- *Co-ordination* – co-ordination is achieved when the leader reconciles personal interests with the goals of the organization. This synchronization can only be achieved through effective and proper co-ordination.

Depending on the structure of the business, the leader also has a role in observing the levels of management. At the top level of management, their job is to formulate policies and plans. In the lower and middle levels, they have to interpret policies and execute programs and plans according to the framing of the top management. Leadership may also be exercised through counseling subordinates about executing their plans.

The leader also works as a representative of the organization. They have to talk about the interests of the business with the people outside of the business in general meetings, seminars, and conferences. The role of the leader is to explain the business to the outside world.

In that sense, the leader must be able to reconcile and integrate personal and organizational goals. They must be able to use their traits to help reconcile their goals and the goals of the employee with what the organization hopes to achieve. The leader needs this ability to solicit support from other people. They need not only make sure that subordinates co-operate, but also help when the business needs to work with other companies.

Finally, a leader must also be a guide and a philosopher. They must be able to be a friend when it matters, to share their feelings, desires, and opinions with their employees. They need to be able to use intelligence and experience to guide employees and secure their co-operation.

Even with the description of what a leader should be able to do, it is clear that there is a difference between a bad leader and a good leader. Most literature will agree that a good leader exhibits any or all of the following characteristics:

- *A pleasing physical appearance* – the leader, must have a physique and presentation that communicates to their position.

- *Foresight and vision* – A leader will only maintain influence if they exhibit their ability to look forward and visualize situations to frame programs.

- *Intelligence* – The leader should be intelligent enough to examine different situations and problems. They have to be analytical enough to weigh various sides of an issue and summarize the situation well.

- *Communicative skills* – The leader needs to be able to explain policies and procedures adequately, precisely, and clearly.

- *Knowledge of work* – a good leader should know the nature of their work and understand their subordinates well.

- *Objectivity* – people trust a leader who displays a fair outlook, free from bias. He should form his own opinion based on logic and facts.

- *Sense of responsibility* - responsibility refers to accountability toward the work of an individual to inspire a sense of influence. The leader must have a sense of responsibility toward the goals of the business. Only then can he make sure that he gets the best from himself and his subordinates.

- *Will-power and self-confidence* – If a leader earns the confidence of other people, he must be confident in his abilities. He should be trustworthy enough to handle situations with full will power.

- *Empathy* – A leader needs to be able to interact with different types of people without any prejudices. They need to be able to handle personal problems between subordinates with great attention and care, through humanitarian grounds. Empathy is a necessary tool for this. The leader needs the ability to step into the shoes of other people to understand their complaints and problems to help them sort them.

The relationship between emotional intelligence and the workplace

Many businesses utilize emotional intelligence tests and training to help develop the people in leadership positions. However, social intelligence can benefit anyone in any field. Consider the following examples:

Leadership and management

Many people possess management or leadership potential based on their personalities. Those who do not have these traits will likely appreciate the wisdom they get from growing their emotional intelligence. They may use that knowledge to better their style of management. Emotional intelligence helps the manager interact better with staff, clients, and superiors.

Sales and marketing

Emotional intelligence can improve sales and marketing tremendously. Professionals learn how to approach people and break down their walls. They will also learn how to use the principles of persuasion without offending other people's boundaries. Highly persuasive salespeople exhibit excellent social skills and can communicate well in the spoken or written word.

Customer service and service providers

Emotional intelligence can help customer service representatives to assess the wants of their customers and meet those needs without even sometimes giving them everything they want. Providing excellent customer support is easy for someone who has high emotional intelligence.

Human resources

Human resource departments often get bad mouthed for muddying the waters with bureaucracy and paperwork, but they play crucial roles in businesses. The human resource person who is well trained can be a go-to person for employees to vent. They can help with communications across departments and make sure that the workplace is liveable.

Administrative support

The administrator may not be the first one to come to mind when you think of emotional intelligence, but they can benefit substantially from such training. These employees will often be lost in the background, but they are the background of successful companies. They run interference every day, interacting with dissatisfied employees, suppliers, customers, and other people within the organization.

Emotional intelligence in a leader

Perhaps due to the manner, that leadership is taught, or due to people's personal biases, the idea of the perfect leader is always someone who is removed from any situation. They have their temper in control and their emotions under even greater control, and they treat their employees with civility and professionalism.

While this image is alright, there is a reason there has been a recent shift in the modes of leadership.

It is no longer enough that someone is removed from situations, communicating only through emails, and ensuring co-operation by threatening to fire you. A good leader needs emotional intelligence.

Hopefully, by this point in the book, you understand that there is no way to fake empathy or emotional intelligence. The effective leader must, therefore, work on himself to become an exemplary person. They need to understand their emotions and those of others before they can channel them toward achieving their goals.

The following are specific areas you must grow as a leader:

1. *Self-awareness*

A good leader needs to know how they feel. They need to identify the ways their actions and emotions affect the people around them. When in a position of leadership, self-awareness is about having a clear picture of your weaknesses and your strengths and being able to navigate them with humility.

- *Keep a journal* – A journal will help you to improve your self-awareness. Spend a few minutes every day, writing your thoughts and feelings about a particular issue.

- *Slow down* – When you experience intense emotions such as anger, take a moment to examine the reason. Keep in mind that regardless of the situation, you can choose what your reaction will be.

2. *Self-regulation*

A leader who self-regulates will rarely attack other people verbally. They do not make rushed emotional choices or stereotype people. They are also careful not to compromise their values. Self-regulation helps you to stay in control. It is about an unwavering commitment to personal accountability.

- *Know your values* – Do you know the particular things that you will not compromise? Do you know what values you find the most important? Spend time self-searching to understand your code of ethics. If you know the things that are most important to you, you will not have to hesitate in the face of an ethical or moral choice. You will choose correctly.

- *Hold yourself accountable* – If you tend to blame other people when things go wrong, commit to changing that pattern of behavior. Admit your mistakes and face the consequences of those mistakes. You might find that you have more peace of mind, and you earn the respect of the people around you.

- *Keep calm* – If you find yourself in a difficult situation, think about how you act. Do not shout at anyone to relieve stress. If you need it, practice deep-breathing techniques to keep calm. You can also try writing down all the things you want to say and disposing of that piece of paper. That is much better than shouting at anyone in your team. It also helps you to challenge your reactions to make them fair.

3. *Motivation*

Highly self-motivated leaders will be consistent in the pursuit of their goals. They have high standards for the quality of their work.

If you want to improve your motivation, re-examine your role in the job you are doing. You can forget why you do the work you do when faced with challenges. Take time to remember the things that you love about your work. If you find yourself unhappy, consider finding out why and making adjustments. Be sure to get to the root of the problem.

Motivation is also influenced by knowing where you stand. Understand the things you bring to the table and be willing to remind yourself of the same if doubt arises. When you have little hope, find something good to focus on. In the face of challenges, identify a good thing and set your eyes on it.

4. *Empathy*

A leader without empathy will not be able to put themselves in another person's situation. Empathy will help you to see other perspectives and to challenge the members of your team to do better. It allows you to give constructive feedback and to create an environment so free that your feedback is received well.

To practice empathy, consider points of view other than your own. Pay attention to body language while listening to the things your subordinates say. Observe for things like crossed arms or biting lips. Body language can help you learn how someone truly feels.

Respond to the feelings of your employees. For example, you ask your assistant why they are late again. They agree with you, but you hear the disappointment in their voice. Responding to their feelings will include assuring them that you appreciate their willingness to work extra hours and clarifying that your frustration is about the particular thing. You could also figure out a way to give them an off.

5. *Social skills*

Leaders who have excellent social skills can communicate well. They are just as open to hearing good news as they are to receiving bad news. They are experts at getting their team members to support their course or to be excited about a new project.

These leaders are also able to manage change and resolve conflicts well. They will not be satisfied leaving things as they are, or letting someone else do their work. They set an example in behavior.

Learning to resolve conflict is the first step towards developing your social skills. You will likely encounter conflict between vendors, team members, and customers. Conflict resolution also depends on the ability to communicate. As a pro-tip, compliment your employees when they do good work.

Benefits of emotional intelligence in the workplace

Developing emotional intelligence as a leader is not enough. You have to be willing to put in the work of developing such a culture in your organization.

When hiring, employers look for many characteristics from prospective employees. For instance, they want a candidate with experience, who is dependable, and can adapt to different business needs. The employer may also be looking to assess general intelligence and to see signs of ambition and logical thinking.

Businesses need to add ways to assess emotional intelligence, as well. A person could be highly qualified in some areas but lacking in emotional intelligence. If an employee cannot self-motivate, for example, they might be of little use to the business.

It is also critical to put in place systems to help employees grow in their emotional intelligence. The following are the benefits you get for fostering emotional intelligence in the workplace:

- *Better teamwork*

Undeniably, employees work better in a team if they have high emotional intelligence. They can communicate better and share ideas openly with others. They are less likely to control a situation and more likely to let others go first. These employees will be able to trust the members of their team and value their input and ideas.

- *Better office environment*

When you have an office where people respect one another, the culture of the company grows stronger. Suddenly, the workplace becomes fun, and people are more committed to the goals of the business. Staff members enjoy working there but also spending time with their colleagues.

- *Adjustments are easier to make*

A company that remains stagnant is destined for death. Any business undergoes changes and adaptations to meet changing market needs and other economic conditions. Emotionally intelligent employees are geared toward improvement. They will find it easy to adapt to new changes and might even welcome them.

- *Increased self-awareness and self-control*

Emotionally intelligent employees understand where their strengths and weaknesses lie. They can receive feedback and use it to grow as individuals. Managers do not have to handle defensiveness when offering necessary and constructive criticism. Self-aware people know what they can accomplish and the time they need. They are more likely to under-promise and over-deliver. Such employees also know how to conduct themselves in high-pressure situations. If a client is unhappy, they can stay calm and positive without escalating situations.

- *Compassion*

Emotionally intelligent employees will be able to display compassion to one another. They can help each other deal with personal issues and connect.

- *Better time management*

A leader is within their rights in expecting an employee to meet their deadlines. Depending on the company, failing to meet a deadline can mean termination of employment. When working with emotionally intelligent people, time management is not a problem. The leader will not need to micromanage his subordinates to prioritize tasks.

Conclusion

Emotional intelligence remains peculiar and confusing for many people because it is difficult to divorce it from the association of intelligence as a unitary capacity. The ideal view that you have by now is that the term is a catchall word for a range of skills targeted at different challenges.

In that sense, there is no emotionally intelligent person, per se. - everyone is capable of messing up their life.

Viewing emotional intelligence in a humanistic, instead of scientifically, is the salvation out of the hellhole of condemnation once one makes a mess. It helps to know the components of emotional functioning, to be able to introspect, communicate, read moods, and relate with patience, imagination, and charity in emotionally charged moments.

For the emotionally intelligent, love is a skill. It is not a feeling. It is will to trust, to be vulnerable and to show generosity and understanding and sometimes, thankful resignation. The emotionally intelligent person will give themselves time to know what adds value to their life and will be resilient enough to make changes. They know gratitude and hope while keeping steadfast before the humdrum of life. They are aware that they will only be mentally healthy if they can accommodate for their inadequacies and those of others while warning them with charm and apology.

If you find yourself sometimes falling short of your standard of emotional intelligence, remind yourself that that is part of the journey. Dust yourself up, collect your lessons, and move on to become better.